COMPANIONS OF JESUS

IGNACIO ELLACURÍA, S.J.
NOVEMBER 9,1930–NOVEMBER 16, 1989

AMANDO LÓPEZ, S.J.
FEBRUARY 6, 1936–NOVEMBER 16, 1989

JUAN RAMÓN MORENO, S.J.
AUGUST 29, 1933–NOVEMBER 16, 1989

IGNACIO MARTÍN-BARÓ, S.J.
NOVEMBER 7, 1942–NOVEMBER 16, 1989

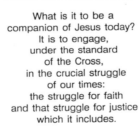

What is it to be a
companion of Jesus today?
It is to engage,
under the standard
of the Cross,
in the crucial struggle
of our times:
the struggle for faith
and that struggle for justice
which it includes.

JOAQUIN LÓPEZ Y LÓPEZ, S.J.
AUGUST 16, 1918–NOVEMBER 16, 1989

SEGUNDO MONTES, S.J.
MAY 15, 1933–NOVEMBER 16, 1989

CELINA RAMOS
FEBRUARY 27,1973–NOVEMBER 16, 1989

ELBA RAMOS
MARCH 5, 1947–NOVEMBER 16, 1989

COMPANIONS OF JESUS

The Jesuit Martyrs of El Salvador

Jon Sobrino, Ignacio Ellacuría, and Others

ORBIS BOOKS

Maryknoll, New York 10545

Second Printing, November 1990

Copyright © 1990 by Orbis Books

Published in the United States of America by Orbis Books, Maryknoll, NY 10545.

The essay "Companions of Jesus" by Jon Sobrino was first published in English by the Catholic Institute for International Relations (© 1990 by CIIR).

For invaluable assistance and cooperation in preparing this volume the editors would like to thank the following: Simon Smith, S.J.; Stephen Kroeger, S.J., for permission to use his drawings; Rodolfo Cardenal, S.J. of UCA Editores; Thomas Stahel, S.J. and the editors of *America,* for permission to reprint the biographies; and James Brockman, S.J.

Manufactured in the United States of America

Library of Congress Cataloging-in-Publication Data

Sobrino, Jon.
    Companions of Jesus: the Jesuit martyrs of El Salvador / Jon Sobrino, Ignacio Ellacuría, and others.
        p.   cm.
    Includes bibliographical references.
    ISBN 0-88344-699-5
    1. Jesuits—El Salvador.   2. Christian martyrs—El Salvador.
3. Theology.   4. Church colleges.   I. Ellacuría, Ignacio.
II. Title.
BX3712.5.E4S63   1990
272'.9'097284—dc20
                                                                        90-41772
                                                                            CIP

Contents

PART III
THE JESUITS AND THE UNIVERSITY

Preface

At 2 A.M. on November 16, 1989, six Jesuits and two humble Salvadoran women were cruelly murdered in the priests' house. Their names are Ignacio Ellacuría, Ignacio Martín-Baró, Segundo Montes, Amando López, Juan Ramón Moreno, Joaquín López y López, Julia Elba, their cook, and her daughter Celina Ramos. They were all cherished brothers and sisters to me, my family.

This barbaric murder has had a profoundly moving impact on people around the world. I personally can attest to the impact it has had in the United States where I lived during the months following the murder. Quite diverse kinds of people, from Christian churches and of other faiths, individuals and groups working in solidarity, but also men and women who do not know much about El Salvador, who when it comes to the Third World have only the stereotyped ideas the media foist on them — "revolutions, communism, democracy" — all these could not comprehend how in a Christian country six Jesuit priests and two women — whose only crime was to spend the night in the priests' home out of concern for their own security — could be murdered so unjustly, cruelly, and pitilessly. The impact has indeed been great.

Time goes on, however, and the initial emotional reaction tends to abate little by little. This is quite understandable but it is neither good nor healthy that events like these, both important and tragic, should be forgotten. It is not good, because such forgetting is dehumanizing for the living, whereas keeping memory alive is humanizing. That is why we must keep these persons and these events alive. We must keep recalling — for the naive or the blind — that such things could take place just a few thousand miles from U.S. soil, while democracy is supposedly sweeping forward around the world. It is very important to maintain the suspicion that our Western world is not so beautiful, free, and democratic as it is made out to be. And for those who are aware, in solidarity and commitment, it is good to keep up this service and to do even more to bring the crucified down from their crosses, as Ignacio Ellacuría used to say. It is in keeping alive and energizing this memory, both necessary and humanizing, that I see the importance and purpose of this present book.

Those six Jesuits are the core of this book, present here in short biographies, some of their writings, and in reflections on them. Their lives function as a "concrete universal" of a whole people of the poor, of a whole crucified Third World, and especially of those who lovingly and freely devote their lives to the liberation and salvation of others. And if it is death that tells the truth about life, their biographies and lives can and should be read now from that perspective, in the darkness of murder of course, but in the light of martyrdom as well.

Through the Jesuits the book also shows many other things. Above all it shows the reality of the Salvadoran people — and of so many other peoples of the Third World — a reality of poverty, injustice, and death for the majorities, a reality that puts to death those who cast their lot with those poor. But also a reality of creativity and hope that generates conversion and is also capable of converting all, including Jesuits; a reality of light that can enlighten all, including intellectuals; a reality of enthusiasm and encouragement that can put a heart of flesh into every human being, including believers.

It also shows the reality of a new faith and a new way of being church, as Medellín proposed, in solidarity at all levels with the poor, striving for their total liberation, within history and transcending history, the reality of a new love, even to the point of surrendering life, a love shown by so many Christians who have shed their blood, simple Christians, priests, sisters, Archbishop Romero. . . . It shows that there is a cloud of witnesses to Jesus, witnesses to the God of life and to the life that God wants for the poor of this world.

More specifically, the book shows a new face of the Society of Jesus, the Jesuits. In their General Congregation in 1975 they reaffirmed the Jesuit mission as "serving faith and promoting justice," which subsequently took shape as the "option for the poor." The Jesuits have changed, albeit with limitations and ambiguities. If any proof need be provided, it is enough to recall the price they have paid for carrying out this new mission: since 1975, thirty-two of them have been murdered, all in the Third World. In El Salvador the protomartyr is Father Rutilio Grande, a great friend of mine and of the six Jesuit martyrs, who was murdered in 1977.

Finally it shows how a university can really be of Christian inspiration, something not at all obvious since universities—like anything human and created—can bring into our world sin as well as grace and can support the oppressed but also their oppressors. The murder of the Jesuits at the hands of the oppressors of this world shows that a university's conversion to God's reign is both possible and real, one that turns toward the poor and puts all that it is, all that it has, and all that it does at the service of the liberation of the poor.

In a brotherly way I should like to suggest to North Americans that they read this book as a "revelation"—that is, as a manifestation of reality, initially the reality of the Third World and thereby also the reality of their own First World, a reality that normally remains hidden, or worse, covered up. That they read it as "challenge," as expression and contemporary sacrament of God's eternal question to human beings: "What have you done to your brother or sister?" That they read it as a call to "solidarity," to open up more to the crucified of this world, and to carry their crosses and also to let themselves be carried along by those peoples, to receive their hope, their creativity, and their faith. That they read it as "good news" since, although the events narrated here are tragic, lives like those of these men and women show that in today's world it is possible to come to be human beings, to come to be believers, to come to be Jesuits, and to come to be university personnel serving God's reign; that in a world of darkness with a heart of stone it is possible to live with light and with a heart of flesh, and that it is possible to experience in one's own life the blessing and joy of the beatitudes—this is the most scandalous truth, but also the most blessed truth this book offers.

Finally, I would suggest to North Americans that they read

the best Christian traditions, in the light of the lives of other martyrs, of Martin Luther King, of Ita, Maura, Dorothy, and Jean, and of Maureen Courtney, a Sister of St. Agnes who was murdered in Nicaragua on January 2 of this year. This is not a call to masochism, but an invitation to build on the best traditions, on those that bear mercy, justice, and love. If all citizens and believers build on these best traditions, that will also mean solidarity with El Salvador and with the Third World, for everything good, both here and there, converges for the good of all.

In closing, I would like to add a personal word. I should like to take advantage of this opportunity to thank all those who have offered their efforts and their solidarity on behalf of the Salvadoran people and their churches, and of the Jesuits and the UCA. I should like to thank Orbis Books for the interest and dedication put into publishing this book. And in a very personal way I should like to express thanks for the countless demonstrations of support and solidarity I have received from many places in the United States, especially in Santa Clara, San Francisco, and Washington, where I have spent the most decisive weeks and months of my life. This solidarity, of which I am a grateful witness, shows quite clearly that the death of my brothers, and of Julia Elba and Celina, has not been in vain, and that like the death of Jesus theirs was true death, on the cross and in darkness, but also, like that of Jesus, true seed of resurrection, of light, of hope, of justice, and of love.

Jon Sobrino, S.J.
San Salvador, March 24, 1990
Tenth anniversary of the martyrdom of Archbishop Romero

Introduction: The Crime

Stan Granot Duncan

On November 16, 1989, the world was shocked to learn that eight people were murdered on the grounds of the José Simeón Cañas University of Central America (UCA) in El Salvador. Six of the victims were Jesuit priests, who taught at the university and who were leading spokespersons for a nonviolent, negotiated settlement of the ten-year civil war. The two others who were murdered with them were the cook for the priests' dormitory and her fifteen-year-old daughter. Ironically, the two had left their homes in the community just days before the attack to sleep at the university because they believed that, since the military had imposed a 6:00 P.M. curfew and had surrounded the grounds, they would be safe.

Following the killings, an international cry arose from diplomats, heads of state, religious groups, and the human rights community to find the perpetrators of the crime. Not since the killing of the archbishop of San Salvador, Oscar Romero, in 1980 had there been such an uproar over political killings in El Salvador. At first hesitant, the newly elected president of El Salvador, Alfredo Cristiani, eventually nominated a blue-ribbon "honor commission" to investigate the murders, and after two months of intensive investigations he announced that eight persons in the military, including one colonel, would be charged. Unanswered, however, were questions as to whose orders the colonel was following and how much influence did and does the

Stan Granot Duncan is an ordained minister of the Christian Church (Disciples of Christ) and a freelance writer.

civilian government have over these and other killings by the military.

BACKGROUND

The murders are best understood against the background of the largest rebel offensive in El Salvador's ten-year civil war. The civilian and military leaders were searching desperately to find ways to turn back rebel gains in the capital city. Even though the offensive had been expected by both the Salvadoran military and the government, when it finally happened its intensity and skill surprised everyone. The rebels showed themselves capable of coming and going in the capital at will and of taking and holding strong positions against army forces. In addition to San Salvador, rebels struck forcefully in several other cities. In Usulután and La Paz, troops sent to pursue the rebels were ambushed and totally wiped out. By the fourth day of the offensive, the military high command met to discuss the future of the fighting and the very real danger of losing the war itself. According to later testimony, two important topics were discussed at the meeting. One was the use of the airforce to strafe the poor neighborhoods, or *barrios*, of the capital city where the rebels found their strongest support. The second was a crackdown on leftists and progressives throughout the city in the hopes of demoralizing the movement. Within days the airforce had killed hundreds in the *barrios* and left tens of thousands homeless. The military had arrested or "disappeared" dozens of suspected leftist sympathizers, "death squads" had murdered numerous others, and eight people at the UCA were massacred.

The offensive itself was in great measure a response to the breakdown of peace talks which had just begun between the representatives of the Cristiani government and the rebel directorate, the *Frente Farabundo Martí Liberación Nacional* (FMLN). According to the Arias Peace Plan, or "Esquipullas II" as it was known, government and rebel groups in each of the conflicted countries were to meet for good-faith negotiations toward peace. There had been two such Salvadoran meetings already. The first was in Mexico City in August, and the second was in September in San José, Costa Rica. Arrangements had been made for future meetings.

The projected series of meetings in many ways had signaled the first hopes for a negotiated peace in many years. The FMLN by all accounts (including their own very secret in-house documents which had been captured) had come to believe strongly in the wisdom of pursuing a negotiated peace to the conflict. In the weeks preceding the talks, they made some very serious concessions, such as dropping their demand for power sharing and agreeing to accept the outcome of fully monitored elections. However, a series of events in September and October soured the mood for negotiations, and by the end of November the FMLN had broken off plans for the next round of talks.

FMLN leaders claimed that government representatives at the talks had refused to negotiate in good faith. They said that, since there had been relatively little fighting preceding the talks, the government's negotiating team had come to the table acting as though the rebels had been defeated and that the task was only to negotiate a rebel surrender. Therefore, the talks were useless, and a demonstration of the rebels' real force was necessary. Another important factor which drove the FMLN to cancel future talks and launch the offensive was the dramatic surge in violence against "popular" Salvadoran organizations, such as churches and unions, by unknown persons widely believed to be linked to the government. During the month of October alone, bombs damaged the offices of opposition political leader Rubén Zamora, a school sponsored by the Lutheran Church, and the offices of Co-Madres, a support group of mothers and family members of the "disappeared." The most brutal attack in the series was the bombing of the offices of the National Trade Union Federation of Salvadoran Workers, which occurred on October 31. Ten people were killed in the blast, including its president, Febe Elizabeth Velásquez. Fr. Segundo Montes, one of the assassinated priests and the director of the university's human rights institute, said in a speech in Washington, D.C. immediately following the bombing that it signaled a "qualitative and quantitative change in the human rights situation" in El Salvador.[1] Two days later the FMLN rebels issued a statement saying, "We must avoid the appearance that our presence in the dialogue be used to cover up the government's responsibility in this massacre, and strengthen Cristiani's mask of a moderate interested in dialogue. . . . Given these conditions, we feel it is necessary to suspend the dialogue." On November 11, less than two weeks later, the offensive, named after Febe Velásquez, was launched.

THE UNIVERSITY

Although the Central American University has an international reputation for its intellectual and academic excellence, Salvadoran government officials and the U.S. Embassy in El Salvador have often spoken of it as the intellectual leadership of the FMLN. Its strong support of a negotiated, rather than military, solution to the decade-long war frequently made it the target of threats and occasional attacks from the military or other rightwing groups. Its residences had been bombed on two separate occasions, and once the entire library was impounded by the government. In early 1989 prominent conservative business persons began construction on a 19-story office tower, which they called "Democracy Tower." The name was criticized by many who argued that El Salvador had only a tenuous relationship with democracy, and shortly before its completion it was bombed by the FMLN, damaging several floors. Elements of the shadowy, militaristic, far right, unable to strike back at the FMLN directly, retaliated by once again targeting UCA. Within a week the university printing offices were bombed, and in the process the only non-progovernment press in the country was silenced.

On November 12, the day after the rebel offensive began, the government took over the independent radio and television stations and began broadcasting attacks (usually anonymous) against "communists" in the church, Archbishop Rivera y Damas, and the Jesuits. "Bring them to the public places and lynch them," said one of the radio announcers.[2] Ignacio Ellacuría and Segundo Montes, respectively rector and professor at the university, were named personally in the threats. Some of the verbal attacks claimed that the priests' support for peaceful negotiations with the "communists" was itself a threat to national security.

During the offensive, in the days just preceding the shootings, troops from the army's Atlacatl Immediate Reaction Battalion were suddenly pulled from active fighting with the rebels and placed on guard duty in the section of the city which includes the military school and the UCA.[3] The Atlacatl Battalion is an elite group organized by U.S. trainers in the early 1980s as a crack counter-terrorism force, and has been frequently implicated in human rights abuses. The most famous was the massacre of over seven hundred civilians in the town of Morazón in 1981, immediately following the battalion's initial training at Ft. Benning, Georgia. A professor at the army training school once joked that "we've always had a hard time getting [them] to take prisoners instead of ears."[4] According to papers filed by the U.S. State Department in the investigation of the killings, all of its officers and most of its soldiers had received extensive training in human rights, some of them within the past year. One of the main places where the human rights training is offered is the Salvadoran Military School, of which the man later charged with giving the orders for the Jesuit murders is the head.[5]

On Monday, November 13, a unit of the Atlacatl Battalion, under orders from the very powerful head of the joint chiefs of staff, Col. René Emilio Ponce, raided the rectory at UCA, destroyed university files, and damaged office equipment.[6] Lt. José Ricardo Espinosa, who was later implicated in the killing of the Jesuits, led the unit. The following night, the battalion, which was by that time stationed outside the gates, entered the university once again and searched the Jesuits' dormitories, asking who was in what building and where each person slept. When they attempted to enter the residence of Ellacuría, he blocked their entry, but said that they would be welcome if they returned the following morning, during daylight, with witnesses watching. They did not return.

That same day, Major Roberto D'Aubuisson (Ret.), founder of the ruling Nationalist Republican Alliance Party (ARENA), and president of the Salvadoran Constituent Assembly, went on the radio and made more threats against the priests and "rebel sympathizers" generally. D'Aubuisson is most frequently remembered for the description of him as a "homicidal killer" given by former Ambassador to El Salvador Robert White during Congressional testimony. He is also known to have fond feelings for the Nazis and their system of solving national social problems. He once commented to a group of visiting Germans, "You Germans were very intelligent. You realized that the Jews were responsible for the spread of Communism and you began to kill them."[7]

D'Aubuisson created the ruling ARENA party in the early 1980s when he came under intense criticism for his alleged connections to the underground death squads. In order to continue receiving U.S. aid and support for the rightist military-led government, he and his colleagues created a new ruling political party using symbols that would be familiar and comfortable to an American audience. They used the Republican party of the United States for their model, incorporating its name in their title, and even adopting the familiar U.S. red, white, and blue as its official colors. It emerged as a "republican alliance" of military and para-military groups and members of the wealthy farming and industrial oligarchy. Its new image has been dubbed the party of the "Reebok Right" for its attempts to emulate an American upper-middleclass look.[8] In spite of these efforts, D'Aubuisson was officially ostracized by the United States in 1984, when it was discovered that he had ordered the assassination of Ambassador Thomas Pickering. A ban was placed on all official U.S. meetings with him of any kind, a ban that lasted until June 1989, when Vice President Dan Quayle paid a visit to D'Aubuisson while visiting in the country.

On previous occasions when D'Aubuisson went on the air and publicly threatened "enemies" of the state, they were often murdered soon afterward in deathsquad-style killings. The most famous instance was the 1980 killing of Archbishop Oscar Romero, who was shot while saying Mass two days after he was denounced by D'Aubuisson in a broadcast on the government-controlled television station. Even though he is no longer officially a part of the military apparatus, and no longer the president of ARENA, D'Aubuisson is still considered "Maximum Leader" of the party, and through his seat in the Constituent Assembly he wields great power. He also still has close and frequent communications with members of the ruling military bloc, including Col. Ponce, the Chief of Staff. Ponce himself has been implicated in numerous massacres, extrajudicial killings, and disappearances from the early 1980s when he headed the Treasury Police.[9] While it is unlikely that D'Aubuisson had a direct hand in the massacre at the UCA, it is nonetheless true that the next morning, November 16, following his public death threats against the Jesuits, approximately forty uniformed men, violating the military curfew and passing through the Atlacatl Battalion guarding the gate, entered the University of Central America and shot eight people: six priests, a cook, and her fifteen-year-old daughter.

THE KILLINGS

The initial information on the killings was spotty, but sufficient to be very incriminating. There was, in fact, a witness who — though she did not actually see the killings themselves — saw the killers and their general movements on the campus. She was Lucia Barrera de Cerna, a cleaning woman, who was sleeping in a building bordering the UCA grounds with her husband and daughter the night of the killings. At about 1:00 A.M. they were awakened by the sounds of grenade launchers, anti-tank weapons, and other heavy power rifles being fired into the air. The men were making noises which sounded as though they were in a fire fight with rebels, but there were no signs of rebels present. What she saw from her window was several uniformed men gathering at the gate to the UCA and a number of others coming through it. When they reached the residences, one of them threw a grenade into the dormitory where several of the priests were sleeping. They seemed to know just where to go, as though they had been on the grounds recently. Two of them rushed into the dormitory and shot two of the priests, Joaquin López y López and Juan Ramón Moreno, while they were still asleep. They evidently were surprised to discover that the Jesuits' cook, Julia Elba Ramos, and her daughter, Celina, were sleeping there also — expecting the curfew and military to protect them — and they too were shot.

After the women were shot, three other priests, Amando

López, Ignacio Martín-Baró, and Segundo Montes, were dragged from their beds and taken outside to the lawn in front of their residence. Fr. Ellacuría, whose quarters were next door to the others, was brought out to join them, and all of them were forced to lie face down on the lawn. Cerna testified that the last voice she heard from the garden was Fr. Martín-Baró's. He shouted, "You are committing an injustice!" Soon afterward she heard another shot and then the shouting stopped.

There was speculation early in the investigation that the killers had wanted to make the statement that the priests were the "brains" of the rebel movement by strewing pieces of their skulls on the campus lawn. While that may have been true, American ballistics experts who worked on the case later pointed out that the rifles used were standard U.S.-issue M-16s, and were sufficiently powerful to accomplish the same effect unintentionally when fired at close range.

After the killers had finished with the priests, they searched the residences, torched the university archives, and threw grenades into the school of theology. Before leaving, some of the men went to several of the buildings and wrote rebel slogans on the walls. One person, apparently in an attempt to incriminate the FMLN, wrote "the *FNLM* executed the enemy spies," and then scratched out the incorrect letters and reversed them. The last act before leaving was to fire a flare into the air which appeared to be a signal to others who were monitoring the assassinations. At no time during the forty-five minute event did the guards at the gate enter the grounds to see what was happening. At no time did any of the other battalions in the area rush to the scene of what appeared to be a firefight to lend support or to investigate. On the surface, at least, it appeared as though most of the military and government leaders in the southern half of San Salvador understood what was happening and did not need to investigate.

The next morning, soldiers of San Salvador's First Infantry Brigade circled the archdiocesen offices of the Catholic Church in a military sound truck, praising the killers for their work. "Ignacio Ellacuría and Ignacio Martín-Baró have already fallen," they announced on the truck's loudspeaker. "And we will continue murdering communists."[10]

THE REACTION

The immediate reaction of the Salvadoran government to the massacre was to condemn the killings and to exonerate the military and government. The official Salvadoran position was that the crime was simply another in a line of rebel terrorist attacks. Salvadoran military spokespersons asserted that without question the crime "was perpetrated as part of the FMLN campaign to defame the army and government."[11] The armed forces released an official communique which condemned the "treacherous murder committed by the FMLN guerrillas."[12] Commenting on the testimony that the killers wore uniforms, President Alfredo Cristiani told reporters, "There are many others who do not belong to the armed forces who also have uniforms."[13] In the U.S., Secretary of Defense Richard Cheney stated emphatically that "there's no indication at all that the government of El Salvador had any involvement" in the crime.[14] As late as the end of December, just days before the Salvadoran government itself admitted to military involvement in the killings, a high level State Department spokesperson was still stating publicly that "the evidence has not linked the killing to the military" and that in his opinion, it incriminated the rebels.[15]

Perhaps the most controversial event to follow the killings was the allegation that agents of the FBI and the Salvadoran military attempted to get the cleaning woman, Lucia Barrera de Cerna, to change her story about seeing uniformed soldiers on the UCA campus. After she gave her initial testimony to the Salvadoran investigating judge, the Spanish and French ambassadors arranged for her and her family to quickly leave the country and go into hiding under the protection of the Jesuit community in the U.S. However, when U.S. Ambassador William Walker heard of the arrangements, he asked if he could send a representative along with her also "to facilitate a smooth entry into the United States."[16] Without telling the Jesuits, the other ambassadors, or the Cerna family, he also arranged to have them met in Miami by State Department officials who took them into custody. For the next six days, Lucia de Cerna was interrogated by two FBI agents and Lt. Col. Manuel Antonio

Rivas, the head of the Salvadoran Special Investigations Unit (SIU) which was investigating the killings. During that time she was not allowed to have counsel present, and her friends in the Jesuit community were not allowed to visit her. She said that they repeatedly accused her of lying and threatened her with deportation back to El Salvador if she did not tell the "truth" and change her story. She said they repeated the questions and the threats continuously. "Then I became scared of these men," she said of the incident later. "I didn't have any confidence anymore. And then I said, 'No sir. I don't know anything. Don't ask me any more questions. I don't know anything.'" When she finally changed her testimony and denied that she had seen anyone the night of the shooting, she was given a polygraph test, which she failed. The fact that she had failed a lie detector test was immediately released to the press as evidence that she had fabricated her story. In El Salvador, President Cristiani held a press conference to announce that she had failed the test and that her testimony would no longer be held credible. The Attorney General stated that because of it she had shown herself to be a "very unreliable witness."[17]

Perhaps the most startling revelation in the affair was that, according to a very credible source, Lt. Col. Rivas, who repeatedly accused Cerna of lying and threatened to send her "back to Salvador where death is awaiting you," may have known since the first days of the investigation who the killers were and who had ordered them to do the killing. The source was Col. Carlos Aviles, the man who finally broke the story of the military's involvement in the murders. Allegedly, he told an American major who works with him in El Salvador that the man later charged with giving the orders for the killings came up to Rivas shortly after the event and told him, "I did it . . . what can you do to help me . . . what can we do about this?" After his alleged conversation with Rivas, the direction of the investigation began to center almost entirely on material evidence (ballistics tests, fingerprints etc.), and military personnel ceased being interviewed.[18]

Following the interrogation, the Cernas were taken into the care of Jesuits in the U.S. who immediately denounced the affair as an outrage. Attorneys for the Cernas demanded that U.S.

authorities turn over the transcripts of the interrogation, but they were refused. To counter the controversy, State Department spokesperson, Margaret Tutwiler, described Cerna's treatment as one of "respect and courtesy. . . . Every effort was made to make the witness feel comfortable and secure."[19] When Cerna's attorneys then requested the results of the polygraph tests which allegedly proved that her testimony was flawed, the State Department stood by its story that the questioning had been handled fairly, but refused to turn over the lie detector results to prove it.

THE INVESTIGATION

Meanwhile in El Salvador, the Cristiani government decided finally to launch a massive investigation into the murders. As evidence of government involvement began to mount, it was becoming more and more difficult to deny responsibility or to blame the rebels. Another factor was that, in what was described as strongly worded terms, the U.S. embassy in El Salvador had informed President Cristiani that if he did not quickly name a person or persons in the military as the guilty parties he would eventually run the risk of Congress cutting back on military aid.[20] To facilitate the investigation, experts were called in from Spain, the United States, and Great Britain, and the blue-ribbon "honor commission" was established to aid the search. Attorney General Mauricio Eduardo Colorado, who wrote to the Vatican demanding that the pope recall priests who preached the "questionable doctrine" of working with the poor because they would no longer be assured of safety, was assigned to head the investigation. Scores of government employees were turned over to the effort, a reward of $250,000 was offered for information leading to arrests, and for two months an intensive nationwide investigation took place. Finally, after a flurry of activity, on January 8, 1990, President Cristiani announced the names of the military personnel who would be charged with the crime and disbanded the investigating commission. He said the investigation had found that in spite of his earlier claims to the contrary, "there was involvement of some elements of the armed forces" in the killings,[21] and immediately made plans to go to Washington to lobby Congress for further increases in military aid.

Because of the almost total autonomy of the military from civilian control in El Salvador, Cristiani was able to announce to Congress that he had successfully charged a relatively high ranking military official with a crime, without at the same time implicating the *elected* government, which officially receives U.S. aid. However, Congress in January of 1989 had been seriously considering cutting back on all aid to countries in the Third World because of budgetary restraints resulting from the expensive 1980s military buildup. Therefore, when Cristiani arrived in Washington he told the president and Congress that new money would be needed in El Salvador to support the military's newly established program of fighting illegal drugs among the campesinos and rebels.

Eight persons were charged in the slaying, including seven who were from the Atlacatl Battalion which had surrounded the university, and Col. Guillermo Alfredo Benavides, who was head of the military school and in charge militarily of that sector of the city. Actually the government's massive investigation did not itself produce the names of the persons who were charged. The actual source was Col. Carlos Aviles, head of the military's psychological operations unit. Aviles worked alongside an American major on improving the generally dim image of the Salvadoran military. The priests' killings had presented to them a particularly difficult public relations problem. Therefore, in mid-December he shared with the major some inside information which he had heard in military circles about Benavides' role in the killings. Aviles said that the information was for their public relations problem, and requested that the major not share it or its source with anyone else.

The major asked him, "Who else knows?" Aviles implicated Col. Ponce, the head of the Joint Chiefs of Staff, Lt. Col. Rivas, who was heading up the SIU investigation, and at least a few others. The major waited for two weeks without doing anything with the information, and then he passed it and its source on to his superiors and eventually to Cristiani. When questioned about it, he said that he held off as long as he could because he was told by Aviles that Benavides and others would soon be charged with the shootings, and he wanted the Salvadoran officials to appear as though they had solved the crime on their own without outside help. When that finally appeared unlikely, he broke the news. The major allegedly had also known, from the same source, of the planned slaying of the priests some days before it happened. He was recalled to the U.S. for questioning.

Many people have questioned the naming of Col. Benavides as the "immediate author" of the killings. For example, the Atlacatl Battalion had been assigned to him at his post at the Military School just two days before the killings, and then reassigned two days afterward. He didn't know either of the two lieutenants who led the unit. It would be extremely unusual for someone to entrust such a highly political killing to strangers. Also he was not known as a hardliner and did not have a long string of human rights abuses, as did Chief of Staff Ponce and others who were not named. Unlike many of his colleagues, Benavides had not been known to make public death threats about the Jesuits. Finally, it would be highly unusual for a military commander of his rank to make such a move without at least consulting with other members of the *Tandona* (or "Big Class") of which he was a part. Renegade behavior was not tolerated in the *Tandona* ranks, and nothing he did indicated that he was acting alone. All of his actions appeared as though he believed he was either under orders or being protected by others higher up. He used military forces which could be easily traced back to him, he promised higher-up protection to the men who did the shooting, and he turned over his operations book which contained incriminating information about the night of the killings. (Not surprisingly, the book and other pieces of crucial evidence in the crime turned up missing during the investigation.) According to the report of the Congressional Task Force on El Salvador led by Rep. Joe Moakley (D.-Mass.), "whether or not Col. Benavides was acting under orders, it can be argued that he behaved as if he were."[22] However, in spite of the heavy evidence of multiple decision making at a very high level in the military, investigators with the Task Force said that the U.S. embassy in El Salvador repeatedly attempted to get them to narrow their inquiry and not to pursue linkages with the rest of the military *Tandona* or the civilian government. That the embassy would ask them to do that, one investigator described as "incredible."

THE EVENT

The actual murders themselves appear to have been decided upon during a high-level strategy meeting of the National Intelligence Directorate the night of the shootings. The meeting was called by Col. René Emilio Ponce, the one who had ordered the ransacking of the Jesuit rectory two days earlier, and who had probably reassigned the Atlacatl Battalion to the area surrounding the UCA. Col. Benavides was also there. The meeting was called because the commanders were afraid that the rebels were about to take the city and that more dramatic measures had to be taken. The FMLN rebels had shown themselves to be much better armed, trained, and skilled than the military had imagined, and the poor of the city seemed to be joining their ranks in much larger numbers than they had expected. There was for the first time a very real fear among the colonels at the meeting that the "Popular Insurrection," long heralded by the rebels, was finally taking place. One decision they made at this meeting was to increase the use of air power, artillery, and armored personnel carriers in the poor barrios where the rebels had their greatest support. They reportedly reasoned that the FMLN would not fight long if the poor people they were supposedly there to help were being killed in unusually large numbers. They also decided to go after and eliminate all suspected rebel leaders or sympathizers and their "command centers," a term used on occasion in connection with UCA. Each person there who commanded a battalion in the various sectors of the city was given an assignment. Some had human rights workers in their sector, some had unions, and one had the UCA. All through the night, following the meeting, noncombatant civilians were "disappeared" or shot by mysterious unnamed "death squads." At about 10:15, during the final moments of the meeting, someone radioed Lt. Espinosa, the man who had led the raid on the rectory two days before. He was asked by someone at the meeting to gather the troops in front of the Military School for an important assignment. At 10:30 President Cristiani was awakened and informed of the meeting. He went to the meeting of the High Command and signed an order authorizing the use of air and artillery power against civilians. The meeting finally ended at about 11:00 with the men joining their hands together for prayer. They prayed that God in his goodness and mercy would protect them and come to their aid in their time of need.[23]

At 11:30, Col. Benavides gathered together forty soldiers in front of the military training school and gave them their orders concerning the priests. Benavides told them that "this is a situation where it's them or us; we're going to begin with the ringleaders. Within our sector, we have the university, and Ellacuría is there." To Lt. Espinosa he said, "You conducted the search and your people know the place. Use the same tactics as on the day of the search and eliminate him. And I want no witnesses."

The group was asked if any one of them knew how to fire an AK-47, the kind used by the rebels. An enlisted man, Oscar Amaya, offered that he did, and a rifle of that type owned by the Military School was given to him. Sub-Sgt. Antonio Avalos, known as "Satan" by his comrades, was asked to join him because he was known for being a good shot. Espinosa turned to the men and told them that their mission that night was to "kill some terrorists who were inside the UCA." At about midnight, they all got into two beige Ford vans and drove to the UCA. They met there at about 1:00 with the rest of the battalion, and at 1:30, they began banging on the university doors.

Fr. Ignacio Martín-Baró was the first to come to the door. He let some of the soldiers in the gate and then accompanied one of them to another gate and opened it to the rest. Within minutes two of the priests and the two women were shot in their beds. The rest were gathered out on the lawns just above the backyard entrance to the living quarters and ordered to lie face down on the grass. Lt. Espinosa asked "Satan" Avalos when he was going to begin. Avalos turned to Amaya, with the AK-47, and said, "Let's proceed." That was when Lucia Barrera de Cerna, from her window in a small house bordering the UCA property, saw the men gathered there on the lawn, and heard Martín-Baró say his last words, "This is an outrage." After that the men opened fire.

The soldiers stayed on the campus for about a half an hour

after that, destroying property, faking the sounds of a rebel fire-fight, and stealing whatever valuables they could find. One was seen taking a valise containing $5,000 which had been given to Fr. Ellacuría just days earlier in recognition of his human rights work. As they were leaving, Sub-Sgt. "Satan" Avalos passed by the guest rooms where Julia Elba Ramos and her daughter, Celia Marisette Ramos had been shot. He heard them moaning and shined a light into the room and saw them holding onto each other in the darkness crying. He then "re-killed" them by firing at them repeatedly until they finally stopped moaning. When the soldiers had finally finished, they fired off a flare, as they had been instructed to do, and left the campus.

When they reported back to Col. Benavides at the Military School, Lt. Espinosa said to him, "My Colonel, I did not like what we did." The Colonel told him to calm down. "Don't worry," he said. "You have my support. Trust me." "I hope so, my Colonel," Espinosa replied.

At 8:00 the next morning, during the regularly scheduled military intelligence meeting in which U.S. military advisors were almost always present, the announcement was made that the hated Ellacuría was dead. The officers broke out in applause and cheers.[24]

EPILOGUE

Meanwhile, many diplomats, human rights monitors, and persons in the religious community both within and outside of El Salvador remained doubtful that justice would be served in the upcoming legal proceedings. During the funerals for those killed, the homilies frequently stated that the real issues in El Salvador were not the complicity of an individual colonel, but a broader ruling attitude of serving the rich at the expense of the poor. "They were assassinated because they sought truth and spoke the truth—because their truth favored the poor," said Fr. José María Tojeira, the Jesuit provincial for Central America. "Nobody can destroy their testimonial to the truth."[25]

NOTES

1. Brian Jaudon, "Decade of Violence in El Salvador: Church Workers Martyred as U.S. Military Aid Continues," *Sojourners*, January 1990, p. 33.

2. "Six Jesuit Priests Slain in San Salvador," *El Salvador on Line*, No. 138, November 20, 1989, p. 2.

3. Just preceding the rebel offensive they had begun a ten-day training course with U.S. Green Berets which had to be cut short when the fighting broke out. The Green Berets were then assigned to pass their time in the San Salvador Sheraton in a wealthy zone considered safe from the fighting. However, their relaxation was interrupted a few days later when they found themselves having to barricade their doors from a contingent of rebels who had invaded the wealthy zones and occupied the hotel. Cf. Rep. Joe Moakley, ed., *Interim Report of the Speaker's Task Force on El Salvador*, April 30, 1990, p. 15.

4. Peter McKillop, "Anatomy of a Murder Probe," *Newsweek*, January 22, 1990, p. 40.

5. *Interim Report*, Appendix C.

6. "New Evidence Points to Coverup," Brook Larmer, *Christian Science Monitor*, February 7, 1990, p. 3.

7. Tom Barry, *El Salvador: A Country Guide* (Albuquerque: The Inter-Hemispheric Education Resource Center, 1990), p. 19.

8. "The Rise of the Reebok Right," Sara Miles·and Bob Ostertag, *NACLA: Report on the Americas*, Vol. XXIII, No. 2, July 1989, pp. 15-23.

9. "Six Jesuit Priests Slain in San Salvador," *El Salvador*, p. 7.

10. "Six Jesuit Priests Killed," *Mesoamerica*, Vol. 8, No. 12, December 1989, p. 3. Cf., Lindsey Grusen, "Six Priests Killed in a Campus Raid in San Salvador," *New York Times*, November 17, 1989, p. 1.

11. "Five Salvadoran Priests Are Slain," *Boston Globe*, November 17, 1989, p. 2.

12. "Cristiani Claims Major Victory, But Capital Fighting Continues," *This Week in Central America and Panama*, Vol. XII, No. 45, November 20, 1989, p. 355. "Murder of Jesuits Overshadows Battle," *This Week in Central America and Panama*, Vol. XII, No. 46, November 27, 1989, pp. 361-364.

13. *Interim Report*, p. 43.

14. Michael K. Frisby, "U.S. Aid: Rebels Gained in Priests Killing," *Boston Globe*, December 20, 1989, p. 17.

15. *Barriers to Reform: A Profile of El Salvador's Military Leaders*, Congressional Arms Control and Foreign Policy Caucus, May 21, 1990, p. 15. The report notes that as recently as January 1989, Ponce apparently lied to Rep. Gerry Studds (D.-MA) when he told him that a massacre of ten peasants in the small town of San Sebastián had been committed by FMLN rebels. When Studds pointed out that the people had all been shot at close range in the head with rifles like those owned by the military, Ponce replied that the rebels had dug up the bodies,

shot them in the heads with U.S.-issue weapons and then reburied them in order to incriminate the army. The statement was later retracted by a Salvadoran Army spokesperson.

16. *Interim Report of the Speaker's Task Force on El Salvador*, p. 23.

17. *Ibid.*, pp. 23-24.

18. *Ibid.*, p. 28.

19. Michael K. Frisby, "House Unit Likely to Probe U.S. on Witness in Salvador Priests' Deaths," *Boston Globe*, December 19, 1989, p. 16.

20. Peter Grier, "US Aid to El Salvador at Risk," *Christian Science Monitor*, January 5, 1990, p. 6.

21. "Salvador Says Jesuits Slain by Military Men," *Boston Globe*, January 8, 1990, p. 1. Lindsey Gruson, "Salvadoran President Announces Arrests of 8 in Killing of 6 Jesuits," *New York Times*, January 14, 1990, p. 1.

22. *Interim Report*, p. 47.

23. *Interim Report*, p. 16. The following details of the killings were taken for the most part from the Report.

24. Douglas Farah, "Officers Reportedly Met Before Priests' Slaying," *Boston Globe,* February 4, 1990, p. 2.

25. Philip Bennett, "Left, Right Attend Funeral for 6 Salvadoran Priests," *Boston Globe*, November 20, 1989, p. 2.

PART I

In Memoriam

∽ 1 ∽

Companions of Jesus

Jon Sobrino, S.J.

I have often been asked to write something immediately after some tragedy happened in El Salvador: the murder of Rutilio Grande, of Archbishop Romero, of the four North American sisters, to name only the most prominent cases. All these were occasions for both sorrow and indignation. But in some way or another, we who survived managed to transform these feelings quite quickly into hope and service. In my case, this took the form, as we say, of analyzing the events theologically. This time it was different. In order to write you need a clear head and courage in your heart, but in this case, for days my head was just empty and my heart frozen.

Now, some time later, as I am gradually feeling calmer, I am setting out to write these reflections. I do it in grateful homage — a small unnecessary homage perhaps — to my six martyred brothers. I am also doing it to try to bring some light and cheer to those of us who are still in this world, a cruel world that murders the poor and those who cast their lot with them, a world that also tries to paralyze those who are alive by killing their hope.

I am writing personally, because at the moment, with my memory of my murdered brothers still fresh in my mind, I cannot do it any other way. Later on will be the time to interpret what happened in a more considered and analytical way, but now I could not do it. And I prefer to do it this way because perhaps writing like this, under the impact of sorrow and my sense of loss, I may be able to communicate a little of what hundreds of thousands of Salvadorans have also felt. Between seventy thousand and seventy-five thousand people have died in El Salvador, but now that it has hit home to me, I have felt something of the sorrow and indignation that so many Salvadorans must have felt, peasants, workers, students, and especially mothers, wives, daughters, when their loved ones were killed.

First, I am going to relate simply what I felt when I heard the news and during those first days, in a very personal way. This experience is not important in itself, because it is only a drop in the ocean of tears that is El Salvador, but perhaps it may help to convey the pain of the Salvadoran people. After that I shall offer some general reflections on my friends and various important matters that their martyrdom raises. I shall speak of them as a group, especially the five who worked in the Central American University, the UCA, whom I knew best. I shall say a bit more about Ignacio Ellacuría, because I lived with him for longer and it was he who most often put into words what these Jesuits accepted as fundamental in their lives and work.

"SOMETHING TERRIBLE HAS HAPPENED"

From November 13 I was in Hua Hin, about two hundred kilometers from Bangkok in Thailand, giving a short course on christology. I was following on the radio the tragic events taking place in El Salvador and I had managed to speak to the Jesuits by telephone. They told me they were all well, and Ellacuría had just come back from Europe and entered the country with no problems. That same Monday 13 the army had searched our house, room by room, and the Archbishop Romero Center in the UCA, without further consequences.

Very late on the night of November 16—it would have been eleven o'clock in the morning in San Salvador—an Irish priest woke me up. While half asleep, he had heard news on the BBC saying that something serious had happened to the UCA Jesuits in El Salvador. To reassure himself, he had phoned London and then he woke me up. "Something terrible has happened," he told me. "It is not very clear, but it seems they have murdered a Jesuit from the UCA; I don't know whether it is the Rector. London will give you more information."

On the way to the telephone, I thought, although I did not want to believe it, that they had murdered Ignacio Ellacuría. Ellacuría, a brave and stubborn man, was not a demagogue but a genuine prophet in his writings, and ever more publicly on television. A little while ago an ordinary Salvadoran woman had said to me after seeing him on television: "Not since they murdered Archbishop Romero has anyone spoken out so plainly in this country." All these thoughts were going through my head on my short walk to the phone.

At the other end of the telephone, in London, was a great friend of mine and of all the Jesuits in El Salvador, a man who has shown great solidarity with our country and our church. He began with these words: "Something terrible has happened." "I know," I replied, "Ellacuría." But I did not know. He asked me if I was sitting down and had something to write with. I said I had and then he told me what had happened. "They have murdered Ignacio Ellacuría." I remained silent and did not write anything, because I had already been afraid of this. But my friend went on: "They have murdered Segundo Montes, Ignacio Martín-Baró, Amando López, Juan Ramón Moreno, and Joaquin López y López." My friend read the names slowly and each of them reverberated like a hammer blow that I received in total helplessness. I was writing them down, hoping that the list would end after each name. But after each name came another, on to the end. The whole community, my whole community, had been murdered. In addition, two women had been murdered with them. They were living in a little house at the entrance to the university and because they were afraid of the situation they asked the fathers if they could spend the night in our house because they felt safer there. They were also mercilessly killed. Their names are Julia Elba, who had been the Jesuits' cook for years, and her fifteen-year-old daughter Celina. As in the case of Rutilio Grande, when two peasants were murdered with him, this time two ordinary Salvadoran women died with the Jesuits.

Then my friend in London started giving me the details that were coming through in international telegrams. The killers were about thirty men dressed in military uniform. He told me they had taken three of the Jesuits out into the garden and tortured and machine-gunned them there. The other three and the two women they had machine-gunned in their beds. My friend could hardly go on speaking. Like many others during those days, he had no words to express what had happened. He managed to give me a few words of comfort and solidarity, and finally he wondered what strange providence had seen to it that I was not in our house at the time.

I spent several hours, or rather several days, unable to react. As I said at the beginning, on other tragic occasions we recovered our courage fairly quickly and were fired with a sense of service, which made us active, in some way alleviating our sorrow by pushing the scenes of terror out of our heads. The Masses we celebrated for the martyrs even filled us with joy. But this time, for me, it was different. The distance made me feel helpless and alone. And the six murdered Jesuits were my community, they were really my family. We had lived, worked, suffered, and enjoyed ourselves together for many years. Now they were dead.

I do not think I have ever felt anything like it. I told the Irish priest who was with me that night that it was the most important thing that had happened to me in my whole life. I do not think that is an exaggeration. My long years in El Salvador, my work, including risks and conflicts, the difficult situations I had been through, even my religious life as a priest, seemed much less important things than the death of my brothers. They did not seem very real in comparison with these deaths. I felt a real breakdown in my life and an emptiness that nothing could fill. During those moments I remembered the biblical passage about the mothers of the murdered children who wept and could not be comforted. When I thought about things in my normal life, writing, talks, and classes, the things I had been doing for the last sixteen years in El Salvador and might be doing in the future, it all seemed unreal to me, with nothing to do with the reality. The most real reality—as I have often written from El Salvador—is the life and death of the poor. From thousands of miles away, and although I was still alive, the death of my brothers was a reality, compared to which everything else seemed little or nothing. Or rather, a reality that forced me to look at everything else from its standpoint. The church, the Society of Jesus, were not for me in those moments realities in terms of which—as it were, from a distance—I could understand or interpret their deaths, but the reverse. As a result of these deaths all those realities became questions for me and, very slowly—and I say this with gratitude—answers too to what is most fundamental in our lives: God, Jesus, vocation, the people of El Salvador.

I kept asking myself too why I was alive, and the Irish priest who was with me asked me the same question. I wanted to answer with the traditional words: "I am not worthy." But really there was no answer to that "why?" and I did not dwell on the question. Instead I began to have a feeling of irreparable loss. The UCA will never be the same, and I shall never be the same. After living and working with these brothers for so many years, it had become second nature to me to rely on them for my own life and work. Whatever idea, whatever plan, came into my head, always ended the same way: but they are not there any more. Ellacuría is not there any more, to finish the book we were editing together. Juan Ramón is no longer there to finish the next issue of the *Revista Latinoamericana de Teología*. Nacho [Martín-Baró] is no longer there to give the psychology of religion course I had asked him to give for the master's in theology. Montes is no longer there to understand the problems of the refugees and human rights. Lolo—that's what we called Fr. Joaquin López y López—is no longer there: he was usually silent, but had a great feel for the thoughts and hopes of the poor persons he worked with in the Fe y Alegría education program. The examples I have given are not important in themselves, of course, but I give them to show that I had lost the direct links that connected me to real life. And I remembered from my years studying philosophy that a writer (I do not remember who) defined—I am not sure if it was death or hell—as the total absence of relationships.

This was my experience in the first hours and days. It was my strongest sensation, beyond any doubt, but it was not the only one. The next morning the people in the course came up to me and embraced me in silence, many of them in tears. One of them told me that the death of my brothers was the best explanation and confirmation of the class we had held the previous day about Jesus, Yahweh's suffering servant, and the crucified people. The comment cheered me a little, not because it referred approvingly to my theology, of course, but because it linked my Jesuit brothers with Jesus and the oppressed. That same morning we had a Mass in Hua Hin with an altar decked with flowers in the beautiful Asian style, with the name of El Salvador written on it and eight candles, which people from different Asian and African countries—who were acquainted with sorrow and death—lit in turn while I spoke the names of the eight victims. That night in another city five hours away by car, I had another Mass with various Jesuits and many lay co-workers working with refugees from Vietnam, Burma, Cambodia, the Philippines, Korea. . . . They also knew about suffering and could understand what had happened in El Salvador. On Saturday and Sunday back in Bangkok, I gave two talks—as I had been asked to give beforehand—on Jesus and the poor. Personally I did not feel much like speaking, but I thought I owed it to my brothers and talking about them was the best possible way of presenting the life and death of Jesus of Nazareth and his commitment to the poor today. Of course in Thailand, a country with a tiny number of Christians, someone asked me ingenuously and incredulously: "Are there really Catholics who murder priests in El Salvador?"

So it was not all darkness and being alone. I began to hear the reactions in many places, the solidarity of many Jesuits all over the world, the clear words of Archbishop Rivera, the promise by Fr. Kolvenbach, our Father General, to come to El Salvador for Christmas, the immediate offer by various Jesuits from other countries to come to El Salvador and continue the work of those who had been murdered, the Mass in the Gesu, the Jesuit church in Rome, with about six hundred priests at the altar, another Mass in Munich with more than six thousand students, Masses in the USA, Spain, England, Ireland, and many more all over the world. I also received cards and telephone calls, full of tears and sorrow, but also full of love and gratitude to the six Jesuits. When they told me about the funeral Mass in the Archbishop Romero chapel, with Jesuits determined to carry on the work of the UCA, little by little I came out of the dark and got my courage back. From what I can tell, the human and

Christian reaction to this murder has been unique, only comparable perhaps to the reaction to Archbishop Romero's murder. Politically there is no doubt that this murder has had the most repercussions since Archbishop Romero's. In several countries, they tell me, nothing has so galvanized the Jesuits as these martyrs. If this has been so, we can say without triumphalism that this martyrdom has already begun to produce good, and this is what keeps up our hope now, even though our sorrow and sense of loss has not diminished.

I have described this experience because I want to say that now I understand a little better what this world's victims mean. The figures—seventy thousand in El Salvador—are horrifying, but when these victims have particular names and are persons who have been very close to you, the sorrow is terrible. I have told this story because I also wanted to say simply that I loved my murdered and martyred brothers very much. I am very grateful to them for what they gave me in their lives and for what they have given me in their death. Finally I have told the story so that what I am going on to say can be more easily understood. I am not going to say anything extraordinary, but things that are well known. I do so honestly and sincerely, not as a matter of course but with the conviction aroused by this tragic event. First I am going to say a few words about who these Jesuits were and then I will reflect a little about important matters that their deaths have thrown light on.

WHO WERE THEY?

Who were they? Many things could be said about them. When their biographies are written, some of them, like that of Ellacuría, the rector of the university, will fill several volumes, because his life of fifty-nine years was prodigiously creative intellectually, in church and religious matters and in politico-social analysis. Others, like Fr. Lolo's, may be shorter, not because in his long life of seventy years he did not do many good things in the San José day school, his early years at the UCA and his last twenty years of direct service to the poor in Fe y Alegria, but because his humble and simple talents made him always want to be unnoticed. There will be such a lot to say about the others too. Segundo Montes was fifty-six, a sociologist; he spent many years in the Colegio and the UCA; he investigated the human problems, especially refugees, he was the director of the UCA Institute of Human Rights. Nacho Martín-Baró was forty-seven, academic vice-rector, a social psychologist who assiduously studied the problems of the poor, the psycho-social consequences of poverty and violence, religion as a force for liberation. Juan Ramón Moreno was fifty-six, master of novices, professor of theology, vice-director of the Archbishop Romero Center, which was of course partially destroyed on the same day as the murders. Amando López was fifty-three, rector of the diocesan seminary of San Salvador, rector of the Colegio and of the University of Managua during the Sandinista revolution, and professor of theology in the UCA. And as well as all these "titles" we will have to mention all their devotion in their daily work of looking after the ordinary people who came to them with their problems, their Sunday pastoral work in parishes and poor suburban and rural communities, Santa Tecla, Jayaque, Quezaltepeque, Tierra Virgen, their struggles to build things in these poor places, a little clinic, a nursery, or put a tin roof over a few poles to create a church. We shall also need to write the biographies of Julia Elba and Celina, perhaps in just a few pages but telling the story of their lives as Salvadorans and Christians, their poverty and suffering, their daily struggle to survive, their hopes for justice and peace, their love for Archbishop Romero and faith in the God of the poor.

I cannot write their biographies here, but I should like to say a few words about what impressed me most in these Jesuits as a group—although of course there were differences among them. I want to suggest what is their most important legacy to us.

Before all else, they were human beings, Salvadorans, who tried to live honorably and responsibly amid the tragedy and hope of El Salvador. This may not seem adequate praise for glorious martyrs, but it is where I want to start, because living amid the situation of El Salvador, as in that of any part of the Third World, is before all else a matter of humanity, a demand on all to respond with honesty to a dehumanizing situation, which cries out for life and is inherently an inescapable challenge to our own humanity.

These Jesuits, then, were human in a very Salvadoran way, solid, not like reeds to be moved by any wind. They worked from dawn to dusk, and now will have presented themselves before God with their calloused hands, maybe not from physical work, but certainly from work of all sorts: classes, writing, the important if monotonous work of administration, Masses, retreats, talks, interviews, journeys, and lectures abroad. Sometimes they gave brilliant performances, as participants in international congresses or appearing on television, in discussion with well known personalities, diplomats, and ambassadors, bishops, political and trade union leaders, intellectuals, receiving international awards. On November 1 Segundo Montes received a prize in the United States for his investigations into refugees, and Ellacuría, a few days before he returned to El Salvador, received from the mayor of Barcelona an important prize awarded to the UCA. They worked sometimes in the parishes, in the communities and in their offices, talking to simple people, to peasants and refugees, to mothers of the disappeared, trying to solve the everyday problems of the poor. Sometimes—most of their time—they followed the dull routine of the calendar—even though in El Salvador no day is like another—working at everyday tasks, meeting the demands of that structure of reality called "time." Through this everyday work they accumulated a great knowledge of the country and the credibility that came from being always at their posts; this gave them great prestige and massively reinforced their work and influence.

They were men of spirit, although outwardly they were not "spiritual" in the conventional sense. From Ellacuría I learned the expression "poor with spirit," to express adequately the relationship between poverty and spirituality. Above all I want to call these Jesuits "men with spirit." And this spirit showed itself, as St. Ignatius recommends in the meditation to attain love, "more in works than in words."

Above all, a spirit of service. If anything emerges clearly from this community, it is their work, to the point where they called us fanatics. But it was work that was really service. In this they were certainly outstanding disciples of St. Ignatius. They did not think of work as a way of pursuing a career. Some of them could easily have been world figures in their professions and some indeed were, although they never directly sought to be. It was not that they did not enjoy peace and quiet. But given the needs of the country and Ellacuría's creativity in always proposing new plans and never letting us rest on our laurels, work is what dominated the community. This had its disadvantages but above all it was the witness of lives dedicated to serving others. They nearly all did pastoral work in poor parishes and communities on Sundays after an exhausting week, and on many Saturday and Sunday afternoons they could be seen working in their offices. I remember, for example, that at times we discussed finishing the week's work in the UCA on Friday afternoons, and not at noon on Saturday, as was our practice, but the discussion always ended with these words: "That's for the First World. In a poor country like ours, we have to work harder, not less hard." In fact even the notion of holidays, never mind a sabbatical year, disappeared from our lives. And although this really excessive workload also had its dehumanizing aspect and effects on health, these men lived this way because they were trying to respond to the countless urgent needs of the situation in El Salvador. I remember when Fr. Kolvenbach visited us El Salvador Jesuits in 1988—a very encouraging visit for which we are sincerely grateful—he recommended, as it was his responsibility to do, that we should not work to excess and that we should take care of our health and strength. And I remember that someone in the community replied that in situations like ours it is necessary to be indifferent to health or sickness, a short life or long, as St. Ignatius says in the Principle and Foundation. It was not that we did not understand or were not grateful for what Fr. Kolvenbach was telling us, but we wanted to stress that the situation in El Salvador—not just ascetic or mystical inclinations—required that we should be indifferent and available to give our lives and health. Whether or not this was exaggerated, these men saw their work as a way of serving and responding to the situation in El Salvador.

However, this work had a very particular aim: to serve the poor. When we used religious language, we spoke of the poor, those to whom God gives priority. When we used the language of Salvadoran history, we spoke of the mass of ordinary people. Really these are the same. We wanted to serve the millions of men and women who live lives unfit for human beings, and sons and daughters of God. The deepest thing in these Jesuits' lives was this service and they really did have a spirit of compassion and pity. If they worked like fanatics and ran very conscious risks, it was because they had a gut reaction—like the good Samaritan, Jesus and the heavenly Father—when they saw a whole suffering people on the road. They never passed by on the other side like the priest and the Levite in the parable, so as to avoid meeting and being affected by the people's suffering. They never said no to anything people asked them if it was possible for them to oblige. They never sought refuge in academic work to avoid the needs of the people, as if university knowledge was not also subject to the primary ethical and practical requirement to respond to the cry of the masses. So the inspiration of all their work and service was this compassion and pity, which they truly put first and last. The language they used as university men was of "justice," "transformation of structures," "liberation," including, of course, "revolution," but this was not a cold academic language, of ideology or politics. Behind it lay the real language of love for the Salvadoran people, the language of pity. With this people and for this people they lived many years. And they all made this people their own, although all of them except Father Lolo had been born in Spain. "Your people shall be my people," as scripture says.

Their spirit was one of courage. They had energy and endurance for everything, for the constant hard work, for dealing with the thousand and one problems that arose every day in the university, strictly university problems and problems that arose day after day in the country and reached the university. So they had to combine classes with giving urgent help to some refugee or someone who had disappeared; they endlessly had to interrupt their writing to deal with calls and visits. There was not much external peace for working and sometimes it seemed that their shoulders were not broad enough to bear everything loaded on to them. But they did not withdraw from problems or let people down.

They had courage to keep going amid conflicts and persecutions. In the last fifteen years they received many threats from phone calls or anonymous letters, and especially in the newspapers, with fantastic accusations in editorials and advertisements—sometimes paid for by the army—which suggested in one way or another, or plainly demanded, the expulsion or annihilation of these Jesuits. In recent months clear threats appeared in the press and on television, especially against Ellacuría and Segundo Montes. The final threats were on the radio, when from November 12 onward all the transmitters were in government hands and issuing threats against the Jesuits and the archbishop.

And as well as verbal threats, they suffered physical attacks. From January 6, 1976—I remember the date very well—when they placed the first bomb in our university, there have been fifteen occasions when bombs have been planted, in the print room, the computer center, the library, the administration building. The last one exploded on July 22 this year, partially destroying the printing press. The police came to our own house four times and on the last occasion they stayed for eleven hours. In February 1980 the house was heavily machine-gunned at night, and in October of the same year it was dynamited twice: on the 24th and three days later, on the 27th. In 1983 a new bomb exploded in our house; this time because we had defended dialogue as the most human and Christian solution for the country. A tragic irony, but in those days the very word "dialogue" was synonymous with betrayal.

So their service to the mass of the people was very aware of the risks. They accepted the risk perfectly naturally without any fuss, and not even through any special spiritual discernment, because one only discerns what is not clear and for these men it was absolutely clear that they had to go on with their work in the country. That is why they remained in El Salvador and I never heard them saying they should leave, whatever the threats and dangers. Perhaps the very fact of their remaining in the country was a great service to many who might have left if they had abandoned the country. In 1977, after Rutilio Grande was murdered, we all received death threats. The names of various UCA Jesuits were always on the lists of dangerous persons. And remember that in El Salvador leaflets were even thrown in the street saying "Be a patriot, kill a priest." Sometimes we spent nights in nuns' houses or with friendly families, but the next day we all returned to work at the UCA.

Only once, in November 1980, did Ellacuría leave the country under the protection of the Spanish embassy, because his name was top on a secret list of persons who were going to be killed. And remember that that year the threats were very real; it was the year when Archbishop Romero was murdered, four priests, four North American sisters, a seminarian, the rector of the National University, the five principal leaders of the Democratic Revolutionary Front (FDR) and, as always, hundred of peasants, workers, trade unionists, students, teachers, doctors, journalists. ... Ellacuría later returned to the country with no guarantee, fully aware that he was taking on all these risks again. There is no doubt that they were brave men, of a piece with the Salvadoran people who molded them and who have given an example to the world of how to bear endless misfortunes, how to survive and how to struggle for life with a creativity that astonishes all those who know them. So these men were true Salvadorans, and I should like to add that the courage and honesty and service with which they lived were returned in full measure by this people. The people's sufferings transformed and purified them, by their hope they lived, and their love won their hearts forever.

These men were also believers, Christians. I do not mention this here as something obvious or to be taken for granted, but as something central in their lives, something that really ruled all their lives. They were not conventionally "pious" types, repeating "Lord, Lord," in the temple, but they were people who went out into the street to do God's will. So when we spoke about matters of faith in the community, our words were sparing but really meant. We spoke about God's kingdom and the God of the kingdom, of Christian life as a following of Jesus, the historical Jesus, Jesus of Nazareth, because there is no other. In the university—in teaching and theological writings, of course—but also in solemn moments and public acts we recalled our Christian inspiration as something central, as what gave life, direction, force, and meaning to all our work, and explained the risks the university very consciously incurred. There was plain speaking about God's kingdom and the option for the poor, sin and the following of Jesus. This Christian inspiration of the university was never just rhetoric when these Jesuits talked about it, and people understood that this was really the university's inspiration. Even some who would have been reluctant to call themselves believers realized and were grateful because this Christian faith lived in this way made the university more Salvadoran.

It is difficult or impossible to see to the bottom of these men's hearts, their faith, but for me there is no doubt that they were great believers and that their lives alone had meaning as followers of Jesus. What was their faith like? Thinking of each one of them singly, with their different life stories and characters, I feel fascinated and grateful above all for the fact that they did have great faith, because in countries like El Salvador faith is not something obvious, amid so much injustice and so much silence from God, and I never fail to be impressed by the very fact that there is faith.

I think they believed in a God of life, who favored the poor, a beneficent utopia amid our history, a God who gives meaning and salvation to our lives and hence a radical hope. I think they found God hidden in the suffering face of the poor and they found God crucified in the crucified people. And they also found God in those acts of resurrection, great and small, by the poor. And in this God of the lowly — God ever littler — they found the God who is ever greater, the true inexhaustible mystery, which impelled them along untrodden ways and to ask what had to be done. I should like to say of them what I have written elsewhere about Jesus of Nazareth. For them God was a good father, history's beneficent utopia, that attracted them and made them give more and more of themselves. In God they could rest and find the ultimate meaning of their lives. But for them the Father went on being God, the mystery beyond our control, and therefore God did not let them rest and drove them to keep seeking new things to do to respond to the new and sovereign divine will.

I have already said that our community was not very prone to put things into words, preferring to say them with our lives. Now my brothers have said them with their blood. But I want to mention someone they often did talk about: Archbishop Romero. And when they did, they spoke the language of faith.

Loving and admiring Archbishop Romero is not at all difficult, except for those who deny the light and have hearts of stone. But trying to follow him and accept all of Archbishop Romero is a matter of faith. I believe that for them, for me and so many others, Archbishop Romero was a Christ for our time and like Christ, a sacrament of God. To come into contact with Archbishop Romero was like coming into contact with God. Meeting Archbishop Romero in person was like meeting God. Trying to follow Archbishop Romero was like following Jesus today in El Salvador. This is what my brothers wanted to do. I do not think that either the Lord Jesus or the heavenly Father are jealous of my speaking like this about Archbishop Romero. After all, Romero was God's most precious gift to us all in these times. And when you feel strongly attracted by a witness like Archbishop Romero, whom we have seen, heard, and touched, I believe that it can truly be said that you are being attracted by Jesus and his gospel, the Jesus we have only read about and not seen definitively.

In any case if it is true that we all feel our faith supported by the faith of others, I have no doubt that our community was supported by the faith of others, by our brother Rutilio Grande, so many Salvadoran believers who proved their faith by shedding their blood, and by the faith of Archbishop Romero. I do not know whether I am projecting on to others what faith in God means for me, but I believe and hope that it is not just a projection. If I have learned anything in El Salvador, it is that faith is on the one hand something that cannot be delegated, like Abraham's when he stood alone before God, but on the other hand a faith supported by others. The two things combine in El Salvador, reinforcing each other. Thus amid so much darkness it continues to be possible, I believe, to have the light of faith. As the prophet Micah says, in a passage I have often quoted, it remains very clear that God requires us human beings to "do justice and to love loyalty." And it is also clear—now in the bright darkness of mystery—that thus we "walk humbly with God in history."

The first thing, the absolute requirement of justice, is what clearly revealed to these Jesuits the real situation of the poor and—in their doing justice—what made them relate to God. And the second, the difficult task of walking with God in this history of darkness—where can we get the strength to do it? I think what made it possible for them was the memory of Jesus, of his witnesses today and the faith of the poor themselves. These brothers joined the current of hope and love that is still running through history in spite of everything, that historical current driven ultimately by the poor. They worked to make this utopian hope constantly increase and gain more body, but this hope also sustained them in their hope and faith. I believe they saw the poor from God's point of view and walked with them toward God. This, I believe, was what my brothers' faith was like.

These men, these believers, were lastly Jesuits. I believe they were profoundly "Ignatian," although they sometimes did not appear very "Jesuitical," if I make myself clear, to those who are always waiting for the latest word from Rome or those who think that the Society of Jesus is the most important thing that exists on the face of the earth. Nevertheless they were sincerely proud of being Jesuits. It is not that they were outstanding in everything Ignatian, but they were outstanding in the essentials of the Spiritual Exercises. I remember that in 1974 Ellacuría and I gave a course on the exercises from the Latin American viewpoint. And in 1983 in our Provincial Congregation we wrote a joint paper based on the structure of the Exercises to be presented to the General Congregation of that year. Normally it was left to us two and Juan Ramón Moreno to put into words what was Ignatian in our lives and work, but I believe the rest of them accepted and heartily shared this vision.

From St. Ignatius we used to recall the great moments in the Exercises. The contemplation of the incarnation, to enable us to see the real world with God's own eyes—that is, a world of perdition—and to react with God's own compassion, that is, "to make redemption." And it is important to remember this because, as for many other Salvadorans, it was not anger—which was sometimes completely justified—or revenge, much less hatred that was the motive force in their lives, but love: "making redemption," as St. Ignatius called it. We also used to stress Jesus' mission in the service of God's kingdom and translate this into our own historical situation; the meditation on the two flags with the inevitable alternative of wealth and poverty, with the

Ignatian intuition that poverty, assumed in a Christian way, leads to all good, whereas riches, by its very nature, leads to all evil; taking on the sin of the world and the concealment of Christ's divinity in the passion, as St. Ignatius says.

Something that was very original and extremely relevant to our situation was Ignacio Ellacuría's interpretation of the meditation on our sins in the presence of the crucified Christ. He related it to our Third World, and asked what have we done to cause all these people to be crucified, what are we doing about their crosses and what are we going to do to bring them down from the cross. From him too I learned to apply the expression "crucified people" to our people. We should not only speak of Moltmann's "crucified God," Ellacuría used to say, although this is necessary. He compared these people with Yahweh's suffering servant, as Archbishop Romero also intuitively did: the suffering servant is Jesus and the suffering servant is the crucified people. Our reply to these questions is expressed with utter seriousness in the conversion demanded by St. Ignatius.

We also reinterpreted St. Ignatius's ideal of "contemplatives in action" as "contemplatives in action for justice." I do not know how much contemplation there was in their lives, in the conventional sense, but I have no doubt that their way of contemplating God's face in the world was in their action to change God's face hidden and disfigured in the poor and oppressed into the face of the living God who gives life and raises from the dead.

These were the Ignatian ideals that moved this group. They put them into practice, with limitations of course, but I have no doubt it was these ideals that inspired them and they bore outstanding witness to them. And this spirit of St. Ignatius is what gives us the clue to understanding how they saw themselves as Jesuits in the world today. They and Jesuits like them are the ones who are bringing about the changes that have taken place in the Society's mission to the world, a change comparable to Vatican II or Medellín, and therefore a real miracle and gift of God. The Society's present mission was formulated as "service of faith and promotion of justice" (32nd General Congregation, 1975), taking the form of an "option for the poor" (33rd General Congregation, 1983). This change has been very radical. For the Society it has entailed conversion, abandoning many things and many ways of behaving, losing friendships with the powerful and their benefits, and gaining the affection of the poor. It has meant above all returning to Jesus' gospel, to the Jesus of the gospel and to the poor whom Jesus preached for and was gospel—that is, good news for. But it has also been a very important change and very beneficial, especially for Third World countries. It has meant that the Society has become truly Christian and truly Central American. It has meant keeping the Society's identity in a way that makes it relevant to our world and giving it a relevance that helps it to rediscover its Ignatian identity. This is no small benefit to the Society, and was produced very largely by Jesuits like the six who were murdered.

Jesuits like them have proved the truth of something else our 33rd General Congregation said: "We cannot carry out our mission of service to the faith and the promotion of justice without paying a price." In the last fourteen years since these words were said, many Jesuits have been threatened, persecuted, and imprisoned in the Third World. I believe the number of Jesuits murdered is about twenty, seven of them in El Salvador—Fr. Rutilio Grande and now the six from the UCA. Although it is tragic, it needs repeating: these crosses are what show that the choice made by the Society was correct, Christian and relevant to the needs of today. These crosses also show above all that this choice has been put into practice. And again this is no small benefit their martyrdom has given the Society of Jesus.

I believe, therefore, that they were Ignatians and Jesuits of the sort the Society wants today. Without fuss, sugary words, or triumphalism, they felt themselves to be Jesuits, again more in deed than word. Certainly it was they who asked Ignatius's two great questions: "Where am I going and what for?" They tried to answer these questions honestly, without dressing them up in florid devotional language or disguising them in diplomatic worldly caution. They did not even cover them with discerning insights that can sometimes be paralyzing, because, as I said before, the obvious is not an object of discernment. They were persons who sought the greater glory of God and remembered Ignatius's saying: "Whatever good, more universal, more divine." This is how they saw their work, especially their university work, which was directed toward the transformation of the structures of their country, so that salvation could reach more people. They were in the vanguard, in the trenches, fighting for solutions to the gravest problems of our time. They were the ones closest to the noise of battle. If they fell in the battle, it is because they were in it.

This is how I remember them, as human beings who were honest about reality, as believers in God and followers of Jesus, and as leading late twentieth-century Jesuits in a Third World country. Of course they had limitations and defects, both singly and as a group. They were sometimes harsh and stubborn, even pigheaded, though not to defend what was theirs but in fighting for what they considered better for the country, the church and the Society of Jesus. But this did not prevent them from living and working in unity, bearing each other's burdens, and supported by each other's spirit. In this way they were companions of Jesus and they fulfilled the mission of the Society of Jesus, the Jesuits, in the world today.

WHY WERE THEY KILLED?

Now I want to try to throw a little light on their murder and martyrdom. A murder is darkness, but *sub specie contrarii* it throws light on many things. A martyrdom has its own strong light, which says more than a thousand words about life and faith. So I am offering these reflections in search of light for us who are still alive to clarify the reality in which we live and give us courage to transform it.

The answer to the question continues to be extremely important, because understanding who these Jesuits were and what they did depends on it. But not just this. The answer also enables us to understand what is going on in El Salvador and understand our faith, which, let us not forget, begins at the feet of a crucified figure who was executed by the powerful of this world. "They kill those who get in their way," Archbishop Romero used to say. And really these Jesuits did get in the way. There is no other explanation for all the verbal and physical attacks I mentioned earlier.

And whom did they get in the way of? Whom did they annoy? Their enemies and murderers used to accuse them of many things. They accused them of being communists and Marxists; sometimes they said they were antipatriotic; sometimes they even called them atheists. They even attacked them for being "liberationists." What an ironical and tragic distortion, to use a term that is central to the gospel—liberation—to denigrate a believer. In fact they did not mean anything particular by these accusations, they were merely expressing their total repulsion and fervent wish to see them silenced, expelled from the country, disappeared or dead. And remember that in this country even Paul VI was accused of being a "communist" when he published *Populorum Progressio.*

Others made more specific accusations: they supported the FMLN, they were its ideological "front," they were responsible for the violence and war, and so forth. This assumes, of course, that the FMLN is the worst of evils in the country and anyone who supports them is automatically a murderer. Of course for the extreme right, anyone is an FMLN "front" who defends the poor and tells the truth about the violation of human rights: from trade unionists who are fighting for their rights and the committees of mothers of the murdered and disappeared, to the excellent *internacionalistas,* men and women who have left behind the peace and comfort of their own countries to serve the poor in El Salvador—even to Archbishop Rivera and Bishop Rosa Chávez and the Archdiocesan Legal Aid Office.

The first accusation is simply false. These Jesuits were honest human beings and Christian believers, convinced that Jesus brought a demand for liberation and the way to achieve it, total utopian liberation. Of course they were familiar with Marxism, its useful contribution to the analysis of oppression in the Third World, and its serious limitations. But Marxism was in no way their principal source of academic inspiration—Ellacuría was an eminent and creative disciple of the Spanish philosopher Zubiri. Neither was it their ultimate ideology for transforming society, nor what inspired their personal lives. That was the gospel of Jesus, and from its standpoint they sought the best available scientific knowledge with which to scrutinize various ideologies and use them in the service of the poor.

The second accusation is not true either. This needs explaining in some detail so that the truth may be known about what happened. This is also to prevent the public from saying—or whispering, because hardly anyone dares at the moment to say it aloud—that even though it was tragic, they did seek their own death. (Things like this have been said in the past few years, even by prelates, when a priest has been killed.) However simple it may sound, what these Jesuits firmly supported and were really committed to was the mass of ordinary people, and nothing else. They repeated endlessly that it was not their role to support a political party or a particular government or even a particular popular movement. Their task was to judge them and support anything in them that helped bring justice to the people. In this too they were faithful to the words and spirit of Archbishop Romero: "Political processes must be judged according to whether they are or are not for the good of the people." Therefore they analyzed and supported what was positive and just in the popular movements, including the FMLN, but they criticized what they thought was politically mistaken, especially purely militarist tendencies abandoning the social and popular dimension, and what was morally reprehensible, especially a few acts of terrorism and murders of civilians by the FMLN. No one who has read the UCA publications can be in any doubt about this.

Regarding the conflict and the war, I remember well that even in February 1981, after the FMLN's first major offensive, which failed, Ellacuría said then that the solution for the country lay in negotiation, words that the right regarded as treacherous and were not very agreeable to the left either. That same year, in May, the journal ECA devoted a whole issue to dialogue and negotiation. Although they were not absolute pacifists, any more than Archbishop Romero was, although they understood and analyzed the causes of the war, its tragic inevitability and possible legitimacy at the end of the 1970s, they were not advocates of war: they regarded war as a terrible evil that ought to disappear. They were fully aware of the good things the FMLN has brought to the country and scandalized the extreme right by acknowledging them. They were fully aware of the creativity, heroism, and love of many FMLN combatants. But this did not blind them to the evils of war, and they were never carried away in theory—or of course in practice—by what Archbishop Romero condemned as the mysticism of violence. With great human and ethical compassion, Ellacuría said plainly: "The way of war has now given all it had to give; now we must seek the way of peace."

Therefore they strongly supported dialogue and negotiation, especially in recent months. The university did everything it could to enable dialogue to take place by itself speaking to both sides. President Cristiani knows this perfectly well. Some of the Jesuits spoke to him several times in private and the UCA invited him to be present on September 19, 1989, when it conferred an honorary doctorate on the president of Costa Rica, Oscar Arias, for his work for peace. In order to make dialogue easier, they spoke to FMLN leaders, with some members of the government, all kinds of politicians and diplomats, including some military officers, but they did all this with the single purpose of supporting a more human and more Christian negotiated solution to the conflict. So they had knowledge, contacts, support for the positive, and criticism of negative things, in the FMLN. There were also talks with some government forces, including support for anything that offered a little light in the cul-de-sac El Salvador is in, whether this came from the government, political parties, or the North American embassy, although obviously they remained firm in their denunciation of the abuses and violations of human rights committed by the army and the death squads, in stating the government's responsibility for these and denouncing unpunished crimes and the useless state of the administration of justice. They continued to unmask the dependency on the USA. So they were not a "front" for the FMLN, or of any other group or political project, although they analyzed them all and promoted the good, whether it was much or little, that they found in them. If they were a "front" for anyone, these Jesuits were a "front" for the mass of ordinary persons, the poor and oppressed in the country. And—this is the tragedy—it was for this that they were finally killed.

These things are well known in El Salvador. I have recalled them here in order to stress that none of the things they were accused of was the reason for their deaths. As in the case of Archbishop Romero, many other martyrs, and Jesus of Nazareth, the simpler and deeper reason lay elsewhere. I mean that those who killed them gave false reasons, if it is possible to speak of "reasons" for such an abominable crime. And of course these "reasons" had no ethical justification. But fundamentally they did not make a mistake, just as, in spite of what Bultmann says, the execution of Jesus of Nazareth was not a mistake. There were no just reasons for eliminating them, but there was a necessity to eliminate them. And this necessity—tragically—is structural and does not derive from the cruelty of this or that person or group. It is the necessary reaction of the idols of death toward anyone who dares to touch them.

There is a deep conviction in Latin America that idols exist in this world. Puebla spoke of them and also Archbishop Romero in his last pastoral letter of 1979, certainly written with the help of Ellacuría. Liberation theology has done what is not done elsewhere, and developed a theory of idols. As has been said so many times, but needs repeating because it continues to be a horrific reality, idols are historical realities, which really exist, which pass for divinities, and reveal themselves with the characteristics of divinity. They claim to be ultimate reality, self-justifying, untouchable, offering salvation to their worshipers even though they dehumanize them. Above all, they require victims in order to maintain their power. These idols of death were identified in El Salvador by Archbishop Romero as the idol of wealth, making capital an absolute—the first and most serious of idols and the originator of all the others—and the doctrine of national security. Then he added a serious warning to the popular organizations, that they should not become idols themselves and never adopt a mystique of violence, even when violence became legitimate. So idols exist, and as Archbishop Romero chillingly said, you cannot touch them without being punished. "Woe to anyone who touches wealth. It is like a high tension cable that burns you." This is what happened to the six Jesuits and so many others.

The UCA Jesuits interfered with the idols *by telling the truth about the situation*, analyzing its causes, and proposing better solutions. They told the truth about the country in their publications and public declarations. This seems such a good and beneficial thing to do and should be praised and supported by all. They said that the most serious matter is the massive, cruel, and unjust poverty of the majority. When, with every right and justice, these majorities organize simply in order to survive, they are repressed. All this continues to be true in the country, although both government and U.S. politicians refuse to recognize it. Their policies do not address this fundamental reality or seek a solution for it.

As well as making this fundamental prophetic declaration, they analyzed the situation and its causes in a way appropriate to a university. In 1971 the UCA published a book on a famous teachers' strike, which supported the teachers' cause. This cost them their government grant. They began to demand agrarian reform as the most radical and necessary solution to the country's ills. From then onward their enemies realized that they were interfering with the idol. In 1972 the UCA published another important book revealing, denouncing, and analyzing the electoral fraud in the presidential elections. This fraud made Salvadorans begin to lose faith permanently in a solution to the injustice coming from elections alone. In 1976, another important moment, when President Molina went back on incipient (and minimal) agrarian reform, Ignacio Ellacuría published an editorial in the ECA journal entitled "My Capital at your Service." From then on he continued to tell the truth and objectively analyze the Salvadoran situation. He told the truth about poverty, unemployment, the terrible homelessness, lack of education and health, the truth about repression and violation of human rights, the truth about the progress of the war, about dependence on the U.S.A., and also the truth about the FMLN and the popular movements, their correct and mistaken actions and strategies. . . . And so many other truths. As another expression of this desire for the truth, two years ago the UCA opened an institute of public opinion, directed by Fr. Martín-Baró, which very soon became the most objective source of information about what Salvadorans were thinking.

The truth, expressed in a university way, is what these Jesuits tried to tell and analyze as objectively as possible. This was acknowledged by countless international institutions, many politicians, ambassadors, analysts, and journalists, who poured through the UCA to hear the truth about El Salvador from these men's own mouths. These visitors did not always agree with all their analyses, but everybody, with the exception of the extreme right, recognized their desire for the truth. So they were not spokesmen of any group or institution, they were spokesmen for the reality itself. If they had or recognized any bias, it was that they saw reality from the viewpoint of the poor. And if they told the truth so decidedly, it was because they were convinced that truth at least is on the side of the poor, and sometimes that is all they have on their side.

Telling the truth, communicating it in a way appropriate to a university, as these Jesuits did, or in a pastoral way, as Archbishop Romero did, has always been dangerous because the idols seek to hide their true face of death and necessarily generate lies in order to conceal themselves. Sin always seeks to hide itself, scandal to cover itself up. So telling the truth becomes an unmasking of lies, and that is not forgiven. The sin of the world, the structural injustice that brings death, is not only unjust but also tries to hide its evil nature, even pretending to be good. It may dress up as something desirable; it disguises reality by using euphemisms: "freedom of expression," "democracy," "elections," "defense of the democratic and Christian Western world." And the world of injustice and power, which brings death to the poor, creates a gigantic cover-up to conceal the scandal of the victims it produces, a cover-up compared with which Watergate or Irangate are small faults or venial sins.

So telling the truth does not just mean dissipating ignorance but fighting lies. This is essential work for a university and central to our faith. If I have learned anything during these years in El Salvador, it is that the world in which we live is simultaneously a world of death and a world of lies. And I discovered this in scripture. As Paul says, the world imprisons the truth with injustice. These Jesuits wanted to free the truth from the slavery imposed on it by oppressors, cast light on lies, bring justice in the midst of oppression, hope in the midst of discouragement, love in the midst of indifference, repression and hatred. That is why they were killed.

The truth they told was illumined by knowledge elaborated in the university, as rationally and objectively as possible. But it was also and essentially illumined by the poor. They accepted the prophet Isaiah's scandalous statement: the crucified people, disfigured, and faceless, Yahweh's suffering servant, has been placed by God as a light to the nations. This is, for those who seek the truth, the option for the poor. This option is not just a professional option, required by the church and the Society of Jesus only of those who do pastoral work. It is a total option that affects every believer and all of us in what we know, hope, do, and celebrate. It is a total option for the church and for the university. This was the option these Jesuits made, in their academic work as in everything else. They believed—and experience confirmed it—that more can be seen from below than above, that reality can be known better from the standpoint of suffering and powerlessness of the poor than from that of the powerful. So their truth was made possible by the poor.

However, the option also means returning to the poor the truth that is theirs, and so they returned to the poor the truth the university generated, to defend, enlighten, and encourage them. The UCA made an option for the poor and put it into practice in various ways. In teaching they tried above all to communicate what the real national situation is—this is the major teaching material, the compulsory part of all courses. This is so that the reality of the lives of the vast majority of ordinary people—the true national reality and not the exceptions and anecdotes about it that are sometimes taught in universities—with its suffering and also with its hope and creativity has a voice.

The question that dominated any research was to discover the reality of oppression and its causes in depth, and actively to offer the best solutions. This was a great ideal, difficult to attain, but one to which these Jesuits devoted immense effort. They tried to offer models, with real possibilities, of an economy, a policy, a technology for housing, education, health, an educational, artistic, and cultural creativity, a Christian and liberating piety, which would make life possible for ten million human beings at the end of this century in this small, poor country of El Salvador. This was the goal of their research.

In its outreach the UCA opened itself directly and immediately to the mass of the people, through its publications, the numerous, brave, and public stands it took, through the Institute of Human Rights, directed by Fr. Montes, through the Information Center and through the Archbishop Romero Center in theological, pastoral, and religious matters. They wanted to help generate a collective awareness in the country, which would be both critical and constructive, and to help the poor. Toward the popular movements these Jesuits were very open and they strongly supported them insofar as they were the people, although not for their particular organizational line. Theoretically and practically they sought to explain the necessity, justice, identity, and purpose of the popular movements. And this was strikingly visible on the university campus itself, which never closed its doors to trade unionists, the marginalized, the mothers of the disappeared, human rights groups, popular pastoral workers, and others.

Where the truth is told, analyzed, and presented in a university and Christian way, this is a kind of university that the idols will not tolerate. They murdered these Jesuit academics because they made the university an effective instrument in defense of the mass of the people, because they had become the critical conscience in a society of sin and the creative awareness of a future society that would be different, the utopia of God's kingdom for the poor. They were killed for trying to create a truly Christian university. They were killed because they believed in the God of the poor and tried to produce this faith through the university.

WHO KILLED THEM?

Who killed them? This question always arises when there are notorious murders. Archbishop Rivera has stated that there is a strong presumption that it was the armed forces or the death squads related to them. The report by the Archdiocesan Legal Aid Office (Tutela Legal) on November 28 concludes after thirty-eight pages of analysis that "All the evidence, taken together, establishes that those responsible for the murder of the six Jesuit priests and the two women domestic workers were elements belonging to the armed forces." It is difficult to explain, in fact, how in an area totally controlled and guarded by soldiers — who had already searched the house two days before and asked which Jesuits lived there — at 2:30 in the morning, in a state of siege and martial law, a large number of persons, about thirty, could freely enter the house, remain there for a long time, murder eight persons and destroy part of the building's installations, using lights, making a lot of noise and causing a visible fire, without being interrupted by soldiers in the immediate vicinity, and leave afterward unchallenged. Furthermore witnesses present have testified that they saw these thirty men dressed in military uniform. Indeed—ironically and tragically—the Jesuits stayed in the house to sleep—despite their fear, reasonable in the light of their experience, that a bomb might be planted—precisely because the area was surrounded by many soldiers and they thought it would be impossible in these circumstances that anyone would dare to make a physical attack on the house. So the conclusion as to who committed the murders is obvious.

But what I want to stress here is not so much who actually did the killing, but who the real murderers are, those who promote the antikingdom and do not want God's kingdom of justice, fellowship, peace, truth, and dignity to become a reality in El Salvador. It is a whole world of sin that has once more inflicted death on innocent people, people who worked for the poor. When they asked Archbishop Rivera who committed the murders, his reply was very straightforward: "It was those who murdered Archbishop Romero and who are not satisfied with seventy thousand dead."

This is the deepest and most challenging truth. It was the idols, the powers of this world, those who do not want anything important really to change in the country, even though they are forced to accept small cosmetic changes because the situation has forced them to. These murders prove that the idols are continuing to commit hideously barbaric acts and get away with them completely. It shows that there may have been a few changes in the country in recent years, but these changes come to a stop when they touch the idols. They tolerate elections, and in seven years there have been five elections, two for president and three for the assembly. They tolerate a few reform laws, which are gradually watered down, they tolerate pressures from the U.S.A. to control the death squads, they tolerate the millions of dollars that the U.S.A. has given to improve the administration of justice—that is, so that it can begin to function at all—they tolerate that the huge military and economic aid be made conditional, so they say, upon their improving human rights. . . .

But it has all been in vain. The idols continue active and recalcitrant, committing ever more wicked crimes. Therefore we need to understand well who really put these Jesuits and so many thousands of others to death. We must not confuse the physical authors of this horrendous deed with the actively idolatrous reality in El Salvador. These Jesuits, like Archbishop Romero, have forgiven those who actually did the deed because "they know not what they do." But they never forgave the idols, but lived and fought to destroy them.

I stress this point for several important reasons. The first fundamental one is that real responsibility for these murders does not lie with the thirty men dressed in military uniforms who perpetrated the crime and destroyed part of the Archbishop Romero Center. There is an "analogy" in responsibility, and even though this is well known, we may recall it here. Of course those who thought up and carried out the crime are responsible. But many others are also responsible, to a greater or lesser extent, through their actions or omissions. Those who cause repression in El Salvador so that justice does not come to the country, share the responsibility for the crime. In the U.S.A. countless persons today rightly accuse their own government of favoring a policy that is incapable of stopping the repression. But it is not enough just to say these things.

What about all the governments in Europe and the rest of the world, claiming to be so democratic? What have they done effectively to stop the barbarities that have been going on in El Salvador for the last fifteen years? What effective words have been uttered by religious leaders, episcopal conferences, universities in democratic and Christian countries? What have the Western media done during these years, when day after day human beings are dying of poverty and repression? Through action and above all through omission, many human beings have ignored, hushed up, or distorted the tragedy of El Salvador. I can understand that for citizens of the First World it may be difficult to grasp the scope of this tragedy, because for those who take life and liberty for granted, it is difficult to understand what poverty and repression mean in Third World countries. Therefore they tend to ignore, fail to understand, and keep quiet. But perhaps they also keep quiet through an unconscious feeling of guilt. It is not possible to keep on living in abundance, having practically everything and wanting more and more, when many millions of human beings are dying of hunger every day. This whole set of actions and omissions is what causes the death of the poor and those who defend them. Therefore the question who murdered them is a question addressed to us all.

I am very much aware, and grateful from my heart, that many persons, communities, and groups throughout the world have shown solidarity with El Salvador, and among them are priests, nuns, some bishops, some journalists, politicians, and academics, many human rights institutions and many Christian or just honest men and women, who have given the best of themselves, their talents, their time, their possessions, even their lives for the poor of El Salvador. Now once more many of them have been expelled or forced to leave the country. As a symbol of them all, I should like to recall the four North American women missionaries who gave their lives in 1980, the United States' most precious gift to El Salvador. They have the eternal gratitude of the Salvadoran people. But for the others, those who are not interested in the poor of this world, but only think about their own interests, "national interests"—as rulers say—or simply want "a better standard of living," without being horrified at the increasing abyss between the rich and poor countries, the causal relationship that exists between the superabundance of some and the dire poverty of others, the freedom of some and the repression of others, for them these murders are a challenge, a call for conversion. For Christians, it is the inescapable demand required to place ourselves before this crucifix composed of the crucified peoples and ask ourselves what we have done and what we are going to do for Christ.

A second reflection is that these murders of priests and Jesuits occurred in the democratic and Christian Western world, as it likes to call itself, which invokes God. Indeed it says it invokes the true God and thereby defends God from Marxists and atheists. We should not forget that Latin America, a Western and Christian continent, is the continent where there have been the most Christian martyrs since Vatican II. More than a thousand bishops, priests, and nuns have been threatened in one way or another, imprisoned, expelled, tortured, and murdered. And tens of thousands of Christians have been murdered for preaching the true word of God, for possessing a Bible or the Medellín documents and putting them into practice. Given this, we cannot fail to ask ourselves what the Western Christian world's reaction would have been if these things had happened in Hungary or Poland, what an outcry there would have been in the U.S. Congress or the British Parliament, what might have been said in bishops' conferences and in the Vatican. But the reactions of the "official" Western world have been very slight compared to the size of the tragedy. It is because it refuses to recognize that the world cannot simply be split into good and bad humans, Christians and democrats on the one hand and communists and atheists on the other. It refuses to recognize that the dividing line in humanity is idolatry, which is present everywhere, among so-called communists and so-called democrats, so-called unbelievers and so-called believers.

At the very least, the murder of these six Jesuits must make the Western Christian world honestly ask itself whether it is as good and holy as it says it is, whether it is as human and free as it claims. The murder should strip off the mantle of hypocrisy with which it tries to envelop democracy and freedom for the few at the expense of repression and poverty for many. It should lead to the suspicion at least that wealth, national security, individual freedom for the few necessarily generate idols who produce many victims in other places, even though these may be thousands of miles away. The murdered Jesuits insisted on this to the end of their days, and I remember that a very short time ago we were remarking with Ellacuría on the absolute truth of the simple scriptural words: "The desire for money is the root of all evil." All those who seek to accumulate wealth and only think about living better and better, should look at themselves in the mirror of the victims of this world and see plainly the evils they are causing.

Thirdly I want to reflect on the investigation that is demanded when notorious murders take place. It is natural that those close to the victims should demand one and understandable that, in some cases, those for whom the political cost of these murders is very high should also demand an investigation, the government of El Salvador and the U.S.A., in this case. But we need to be clear about what demanding and pursuing an exhaustive investigation means in El Salvador. There have been seventy thousand murders and the only ones that have been solved — even then superficially and not in depth — are the murders of the four North American sisters and perhaps one other person. The case of Rutilio Grande, in spite of the promises of the president of the day, Molina, still has not been solved. The case of the five leaders of the Democratic Revolutionary Front (FDR), who were hauled out of the Jesuit school and killed in broad daylight, still has not been solved. The case of Archbishop Romero, although it has been investigated so much, is still notoriously unsolved. And if this happens in famous cases, it is easy to imagine what happens when unknown campesinos are murdered, thousands of them, sometime in great massacres, as in El Mozote and Sumpul. . . . And this despite the fact that many human rights institutions have given important leads on the culprits. Various human rights organizations in El Salvador do this. Among them, with admirable objectivity, are the Archdiocesan Legal Aid Office (Tutela Legal) and the UCA Institute of Human Rights. International institutions also provide information, Amnesty International in London, Americas' Watch in New York, CODEHUCA in San José, Costa Rica. For several years the UN special envoy, Pastor Ridruejo, has also been doing so, and in his recent report a few days ago he noted a worsening of human rights and an increase in torture in El Salvador. In special cases, when the murder victims are foreigners, as in the case of the murder of the Swiss Jurg Weiss and the French doctor Madeleine, there have been thorough investigations by representatives from the victims' own countries, which have given more than sufficient information to find the culprits.

Nevertheless, in spite of all this information, with so many important clues and leads, the administration of justice in El Salvador has done very little serious investigating indeed. Moreover, when the first government junta in 1979 appointed a special investigatory commission, it resigned as a body a few weeks later, when the second military junta of military and Christian Democrats came to power, because as a commission they were unable to do anything serious and they had a well-founded suspicion that those responsible for the crimes would never be brought to justice. Certainly some members of the commission had to leave the country. And on other occasions lawyers or judges conducting important cases were also threatened and had to abandon them.

So what is the point of the investigation into the murder of the Jesuits? Hitherto investigations have achieved very little. Let us hope that this case will be investigated and the other seventy thousand too, of course. Let us also hope that those who are now promising an investigation in order to convey a sense of normality and democracy, first investigate why there have not been and could not have been any serious investigations in El Salvador. And let us hope they investigate why the vast majority of victims of notorious crimes — and also of course of the less well-known crimes — happen to be persons devoted to defending the poor.

Personally I have begun to be fed up with the very word "investigation." In our community when successive governments announced that they were conducting "an exhaustive investigation" into a notorious crime, we used to comment ironically that a simple, normal, rapid investigation would do because the "exhaustive" investigations never come to an end. Let us hope that promises of investigation do not become an elegant excuse not to stop the repression. And let us hope the investigation of this case, if it is carried through to the end and those responsible are brought to justice, does not become a cover-up to distract attention from the seventy thousand cases also needing investigation, and does not become that most bitter of ironies, an excuse for saying that things are getting better in El Salvador.

The word "investigation" has gone the way of other noble words like "democracy" and "elections." They say little or nothing, and are often used for the opposite of what they mean. Personally I sometimes think it is better that there should not be an investigation, and that it goes down in history that the murderer of Archbishop Romero and thousands of Christians was the sin of the world, the antikingdom, the idols. Because it is much more important to repeat and proclaim this great truth than to find out one day the name of the actual killer. And it is important not to let the idols and those who support them ease their consciences because, after all now, it is known who pulled the trigger.

My fourth reflection is necessary. If it is possible to kill with impunity these well-known and respected Jesuits, some of them with international reputations, even when it was easy to foresee the world reaction that is now taking place, the high political cost, international pressures, if none of this could hinder the barbarity of murdering six priests, it is not difficult to imagine what defense peasants hidden away in little villages and country districts might have. Practically none. Even though it is obvious, it needs repeating. Who in the world is really working to stop this from happening and demanding an investigation of the El Mozote and Sumpul massacres, or the most recent one, on October 31, 1989, when ten trade unionists were murdered in broad daylight? This time the names of the two ordinary women who were killed are known, Julia Elba and Celina; their deaths are being investigated together with the Jesuits'. But countless others remain anonymous and their deaths are not investigated. As the Lord Jesus said, if they do these things with green wood, what will they do with dry wood?

My last reflection is something that has often come to my mind in thinking about Archbishop Romero. Of course it is important for the country to solve his case if this shows a desire for the truth and acts as some check on future possible murders. But I often have the feeling that investigating his case, and now that of the Jesuits, is like walking around corpses without any interest at all in what these murder victims were in their lives or bequeathed to us. The El Salvador and U.S. governments are talking now about investigating the case of the six Jesuits. Let us hope they do it. But is it not much more important for the country to remember what they did in their lives and to keep their spirit present?

The poor of El Salvador weep for their dead but what they want above all is that what they gave their lives for should remain alive. Is it not more important to keep these martyrs alive than to investigate their corpses? Is it not much more important for the country to hold on to the truth, mercy, justice, and dignity for which they lived than to discover the names of their murderers? The latter is not at all easy, as we know, but the former is much more difficult and more necessary. Let us hope—dream—that one day the Salvadoran government, the

U.S. government and congress act on what these men were in their lives, seriously study the solution they proposed for the country, recognize the truth as they analyzed it, acknowledge that without justice and without respect for human rights there can be no solution—with or without elections. These martyrs do not seek revenge, they are not even concerned with obtaining justice for themselves. What they want is that peace and justice should come to El Salvador, and that in order for this to happen we should follow the best ways they showed us.

These are the reflections that come to my mind in connection with the murder of my six brother Jesuits. It is important to know who killed them, but more important to know why it is possible to murder them with such impunity, before, during, and after the event. It is important to investigate the murders of the past, but much more important once and for all to stop murders happening in the future. It is important to solve notorious murders but more important to clear up the mass murder of peasants who die anonymously. It is important that justice should be done to my brother Jesuits in death, but it is much more important to keep them present by trying to keep what they were and did during their lives.

A NEW IDEA OF A CHRISTIAN UNIVERSITY

These dark and tragic murders reveal some very important things. There are idols in this world and they produce victims; there is sin and it produces death. But when as well as murder it is martyrdom—there have been thousands in El Salvador—it testifies to what is the most important thing in our lives. With death we tell the truth about our lives and by their death these Jesuits told the truth about what they were and did. And because they died a martyr's death, this also confirms that what they were and did was true. So now although it may seem a digression, I should like to mention three important things their martyrdom throws light on. What is a Christian university? What is the church of the poor and liberation theology? These subjects are important, topical, and disputed. They need illuminating and here these Jesuits bequeathed us an important legacy.

What kind of university did they leave us? Above all, they

left us a new idea of a Christian university for our time, comparable in importance to that of John Henry Newman a century ago—and also many models of this new Christian university. When I was speaking about why they were killed, I said a little about what the UCA meant to them—ideally, of course, but also in many of its actual doings. In a word, what they left us was the belief that academic and Christian knowledge must be and can be at the service of the poor.

They wrote a great deal about this idea of a new Christian university in the service of the poor. And although I have avoided long quotations, allow me one exception, a quotation from Ignacio Ellacuría's speech when he received an honorary doctorate from Santa Clara University, California, in 1982.

> The starting point of our conception of what a university should be consists of two considerations. The first and most obvious is that the university has to do with culture, knowledge, a particular exercise of intellectual reason. The second consideration, which is not so obvious and commonplace, is that the university is a social reality and a social force, historically marked by what society is like in which it lives. As a social force, it should enlighten and transform that reality in which it lives and for which it should live....
>
> Our intellectual analysis finds that our historical reality, the reality of El Salvador, the reality of the Third World— that is, the reality of most of this world, the most universal historical reality—is fundamentally characterized by the effective predominance of falsehood over truth, injustice over justice, oppression over freedom, poverty over abundance—in sum, of evil over good....
>
> This is the reality with which we live and have to cope, and we ask ourselves what to do about it in a university way. We answer, first, from an ethical standpoint: we must transform it, do all we can to ensure that good predominates over evil, freedom over oppression, justice over injustice, truth over falsehood, and love over hatred. If a university does not decide to make this commitment, we do not understand the validity it has as a university,

much less as a Christian-inspired university. . . .

A Christian-inspired university focuses all its academic activity according to what it means to make a Christian preferential option for the poor. . . . The university should become incarnate among the poor, it should become science for those who have no science, the clear voice of those who have no voice, the intellectual support of those whose very reality makes them true and right and reasonable, even though this sometimes takes the form of having nothing, but who cannot cite academic reasons to justify themselves.

Our university has modestly tried to adopt this difficult and conflictive course. It has obtained some results through its investigations, publications, denunciations; particularly through certain persons who have abandoned other more brilliant, worldly, and lucrative alternatives to devote themselves to making a university contribution to the liberation of the Salvadoran people; sometimes through students and staff who have paid very painfully with their own lives, exile, ostracism, for their dedication to the university's service of the oppressed majorities. . . .

For this work we have been severely persecuted. . . . If our university had suffered nothing during these years of passion and death for the Salvadoran people, it would mean it had not fulfilled its mission as a university, never mind displaying its Christian inspiration. In a world where falsehood, injustice, and oppression reign, a university that fights for truth, justice and freedom cannot fail to be persecuted.

There in few and lucid words is what these men thought about what a Christian university in the Third World should be. They arrived at this conclusion not just through theoretical reflection but also through historical experience of what a university in the Third World is. Therefore they were very much aware of the possibilities and also the danger of a university aimed at extending God's kingdom. Perhaps it sounds odd, but they were very aware that a university is also threatened by sinfulness, that it can serve the antikingdom, or more particularly, it can reinforce through the professionals it produces and through its social position the unjust structures in a society. Not only can a university do this, but it frequently does so and introduces sin into society. Therefore these Jesuits were not at all naive about the possibilities of a university, but critical. They believed that, like any other human body, the university and its specific instrument, rational knowledge, is also threatened with sinfulness, and therefore that a Christian-inspired university must above all be a converted university. Conversion means putting all its social weight through its specific instrument, rational knowledge, at the service of the oppressed majorities. This is what these men wanted to do and did: in a university and Christian way, they made an option for the poor.

So the final lesson remains—and perhaps it may be useful now when a document is being drawn up in the Vatican on Catholic universities—that a Christian university is possible in the Third World, a university that is not isolated as an ivory tower and stonehearted toward the suffering of the poor, but a university sharing bodily in their suffering and hopes, a university with a heart of flesh. Another unforgettable lesson is that any Christian activity, including academic activity, is done in the presence of the antikingdom, which is opposed to it and fights against it. In the case of a university, this may take the form of lies. The lesson remains that—as always happens, from the prophets onward, from Jesus onward—stating and analyzing the truth means defending the poor and therefore confronting oppressors. The lesson remains, the most important lesson that was these men's life, that a university can be the voice of the poor; it can keep up their hope and help them on their way to liberation.

And we are left with the supreme lesson, that of the greatest love. Tragically, throughout history those who proclaim God's kingdom have to confront the antikingdom. It does not matter whether they do it as peasants, workers, nuns, priests, bishops, professionals, or academics; they are all persecuted. These university Jesuits were also killed for defending the poor. And if the magnitude of the attack is in proportion to their defense of the poor, then we can say that the UCA defense of the poor has been firm indeed.

THEIR CHURCH

What kind of a church did they leave us? It is a difficult and even polemical matter to speak of the church today. The reader will understand that it is not at all my intention and neither is this the moment to enter into polemic or defend interests. It is a moment for sincerity before God and ourselves. Therefore in the presence of their corpses, I want to consider calmly the perennial and fundamental problem, raised again by Vatican II and Medellín, of what is the true church of Jesus and what followers of Jesus, who are members of his body in history, should be like in our world today.

At the funeral Mass in the presence of the six corpses, the papal nuncio called them true sons and members of the church. And he gave them the name reserved by the church for her finest children: martyrs. He is completely right, because they really were ecclesial. I have often said, sincerely and without irony, that although as is well known there have been many tensions between Jesuits and some members of the hierarchy, we Central American Jesuits have become more ecclesial in these recent years. The reason for this is that now we are more integrated within the people of God, we share more of their real life, we feel ourselves to be less elitist and triumphalist, more supported by the faith, hope, and love of others, especially of the poor, the people of God. We are able to follow Christ better, and make him present in history, as we are his body making him present in the world as a sacrament of salvation. This is the church given to us by Vatican II, to which we try to be faithful. Medellín stated very clearly that the poor offer the church the greatest challenge. The church cannot refuse to listen to them, it must live and die for their total liberation; in a word, the church must be converted and become the church of the poor. To that church too we want to be faithful.

This is the church the six Jesuits belonged to, which they also officially represented in their strictly priestly work. This, above all, is the church they wanted to build. In this church they lived and enjoyed themselves but also suffered. The church hurt them when it did not measure up to circumstances, when it looked more to its own interest as an institution than to the suffering of the people, when some of its officials lacked understanding and were indifferent to the suffering of the people, rejecting their best aspirations, when—incomprehensibly—they silenced Archbishop Romero. On the whole the Jesuits thought the church is turning in on itself, that little by little it has tried to silence Vatican II, Medellín, Archbishop Romero, the ecclesial base communities, religious life in Latin America. And how they suffered because of this! That is also why they were critical within the church, of course in a free and mature way, and they thought that prophetic denunciation within the church was a great and indispensable service to it, whereas adulation and servility—which are always rewarded—were grave wrongs done to the church. In a word, they knew they belonged to the church, they wanted the best for the church and above all, they wanted and worked to build the best possible church for the Salvadoran people.

If I recall these things, it is because their martyrdom helps us all to clarify and solve a serious church problem, which is growing rather than diminishing. For some years now, particularly in Latin America, an old problem has resurfaced: What is the true church? We are not talking about it now in dogmatic terms, of course, but in operational terms. It is not very clear by what actual name the true church is officially called today. It tends to be along the lines of "communion" effectively understood as submission from below upward. Its "mystery" is rightly stressed. But the term "People of God" is discredited and suspect. This way of talking enables the church to detach itself from the historically lowly, the poor. Thus it withdraws from seeking inspiration from the poor, from the spirit of the beatitudes, the light that shines from Yahweh's suffering servant. Although such a church does some good to the poor, it does not make them central within it, or see service to them as its central mission.

On the other hand, in Latin America we have the expression "church of the poor," the church that makes the poor of this world central to its mission and shape. This church of the poor is treated with suspicion when it is called the "popular church," meaning a dangerous and mistaken way to be a church, in order to discredit or condemn it. We all know this and many suffer for it. We suffer because this church is often condemned by those who do not know it and are unwilling to converse with it. Above all, we suffer because it is not recognized or gratefully accepted that this church of the poor, with all its limitations and mistakes, is producing a great deal of faith, much hope, much love, and much martyrdom.

I say all this now without bitterness and with the hope that these six new martyrs, together with so many others, may make us all reflect. These murdered Jesuits enjoyed the friendship and respect of some — very few — brother bishops. Certainly they were intimate friends and close collaborators with Archbishop Romero and they often collaborated fraternally with Archbishop Rivera. Bishops like Pedro Casaldáliga have been in our house and felt at home there. Catholic bishops and bishops from Protestant sister churches visited us in the UCA and we conversed in a friendly and Christian way as members of the people of God and the church of Jesus, each with his own function and specific charism. But in some way these Jesuits were also seen as members and representatives of a supposedly dangerous church, one that was disobedient, suspect, perhaps even unorthodox. In their pastoral work as priests they were accepted in the archdiocese and some of them were invited, exceptionally, to give talks and retreats to other priests. But as a whole they were not very well regarded by many bishops in El Salvador and in Central America. Their ideas, their theology, their commitment were suspect. None of them, not Ignacio Ellacuría, nor Amando López, nor Juan Ramón Moreno — to name the three who were professional theologians — were normally invited to offer their theological ideas, useful though they were for the country's grave problems and those of the Central American region as a whole. One Salvadoran bishop, now retired, publicly accused us UCA Jesuits of being the cause of all the evils, including the violence, in the country. Through caution in some cases, through positive rejection or disagreement with them in others, these men who had much to offer the church were ignored and sometimes even attacked from within. They came under suspicion of belonging to the "popular church" or of exercising a so-called parallel magisterium.

Again, without any harshness or bitterness, I should like these martyrs, together with so many other Christians, to help us reflect on this burning Latin American issue: What is the true church of Jesus? In order to decide, we can and should use various criteria: communion with the hierarchy, orthodox formulation of the faith, and so on. But it would be dangerous and fundamentally absurd if other more fundamental and primary criteria were not also used to judge what the essence of the church is. Does not the true church exist when—as well as communion from below with the hierarchy—there is also communion from above with the people of God, the poor of this world, those really preferred by God? Does not the true church exist where, as well as traditional sacramental and apostolic practices, there is a determined effort to preach the gospel to the poor, to communicate and put into practice God's good news for them, solidarity and commitment to them, to the point of sharing their cross? Does the true church not exist when—as well as obedience and faithfulness to what has been handed down by tradition—persons are obedient and faithful primarily to God's will for today, even to the point of giving their lives?

I have formulated all this as a rhetorical question because the answer is obvious. We do not have to choose between the things I have mentioned, but it is important to stress what has priority. To serve the church and the hierarchical church is important for a Christian and a Jesuit of course, and these men always did any work they were asked to do. But we should not forget something even more obvious and fundamental: that the church is the sacrament of something greater than itself, a sacrament of the kingdom of God and the God of the kingdom. Our final loyalty cannot be to the church, but in the church to God and the poor, because God is greater than the church. Telling the poor the good news is the reason why the church exists at all, as Paul VI beautifully put it in his exhortation *Evangelii Nuntiandi.*

This produces tensions, as we all know, which we must endure honestly and fully with charity and hope. However, that should not make us lose clarity. We truly love and serve the church when, within it, we decenter it in favor of the kingdom of God, when we make the church a sacrament of something greater than itself, when it becomes a sign of God's kingdom and wholly devoted to the poor of this world, for whom the kingdom of God exists. This is what these Jesuits' life in the church was about, and the lives of so many others. This, although many will not accept it, is their greatest contribution to the church. This is what makes them awkward, of course, but their shake-up of the church is not to destroy it, as some indeed claimed, or to weaken or attack it. On the contrary, it is to help it become more the church of Jesus.

This church, as I have said, is commonly called the church of the poor, and pejoratively, the popular church or parallel church. I do not wish to deny that there are exaggerations or mistakes in this way of being the church, sometimes an excessive politicization or dependence on popular political movements. This occurs more in some of its leaders than among the ordinary Christians who make up the base communities. In fact, this problem has been discussed in some of the UCA publications with criticism of what appeared to need criticizing.

But this being said, even admitting the limitations and mistakes of the church of the poor, there is something that cannot be ignored and it would be dangerous and wrong to do so, and for the institutional church itself. This church of the poor is the most active and creative church, it is the most involved in the people's just causes, it is the church that does the most in the community to overcome the endemic evil of individualism, including religious individualism. It is the church that arouses the most hope to overcome resignation, that does most to unite what is Salvadoran and what is Christian, and certainly the church that generates the most mercy, justice, commitment, and love for the suffering people. If we are seeking criteria and want to know how the church behaves, we cannot ignore these realities.

Another thing that cannot be ignored is that this church has been ferociously persecuted; it has generously shed its blood and produced innumerable martyrs, who are the proof of the greatest love. And if the end of life is what expresses the deepest truth about life itself, it cannot be denied that in this way of being a church there has been much that is Christian. If so many have died like Jesus, it is because so many lived like Jesus. This is what is illustrated in the life and death of Archbishop Romero, the murdered priests and nuns, so many ordinary Christians, catechists, preachers of the word, members of base communities, and now these six Jesuits.

It would be tragic for the building of the kingdom of God and the building of the real church to take as a criterion of truth what is important but secondary, and to spurn what is primary and essential. We all know this but need to remind ourselves of it. El Salvador and all Latin America have given proofs of incredible faith and incredible love. There are countless martyrs in our countries, and if this greatest love is not a criterion of what makes a true church, we may well ask what is. Let us recall that not all members of the church have been persecuted; many have been favored and flattered by oppressors. The ones most like Jesus were the ones who were persecuted, those who, like Jesus, truly opted for the poor. And that is why the persecution takes no account of denominations: Catholics, Lutherans, Episcopalians, Baptists, Mennonites — all have suffered persecution when they served the poor.

Let us say in conclusion that these murdered Jesuits felt a deep affection for the church. Is this not the moment, in the presence of this new bloodshed, together with the blood of so many priests and nuns in Latin America, and above all in the presence of the blood shed by so many Christians in the communities in Latin America, to reaffirm the church of the poor? It is urgent and necessary for the good of the poor, and the church itself, to point out once more with serenity, truth, and justice the anomalous situation in which a church that is more committed and producing so many martyrs is suspect, whereas the church groups with little commitment are not persecuted at all and not suspect at all either. It is urgent and necessary that there should be dialogue within the church, a calm, friendly dialogue in which all are prepared honestly to admit their own failings, and in which all are open to the love of those who shed their blood. We owe it to them and on them we will be able to build a church that is a true communion and a true church of the poor.

THEIR THEOLOGY

What theology did they leave us? Let us say a little about liberation theology too. Clearly this is not the moment for a stubborn defense of one's own interest, but a moment to reflect deeply on the truth of things and theology. Let us not forget that one of the murdered men, Ignacio Ellacuría, was a well-known theologian, and so too were Amando López and Juan Ramón Moreno. They all tried to do liberation theology. In order to grasp what light their martyrdom can throw on theology, let us recall the type of objections commonly made to it, again not in a polemical spirit but a spirit of calm reflection.

As is well known, this theology has long been criticized and, fortunately, the first to criticize it were the powerful of this world. With great perspicacity—from their point of view—it was severely criticized and attacked in influential U.S. analyses, from the Rockefeller report to the two Santa Fe reports written by advisers of Reagan. It was also criticized later by CELAM and the Vatican in its first instruction, though it softened its criticism in its second instruction. All this is well known and I will not go into it here, because there have already been many replies, and Ignacio Ellacuría wrote an excellent, long article in response to the first instruction.

I would rather discuss here other charges against liberation theology, some well-intentioned, some ill-informed, and some based on total misunderstanding, more a reaction of self-defense against the questions raised by this theology. I think that this is a good way to get to the essence of liberation theology.

Some say that liberation theology is not scientific enough, that of course it is inspired by faith but it is uncritical and even naive. Others, on the contrary, say that liberation theology is basically elitist, an academic pursuit that does not reach the great majority. Many say, or imply, that liberation theology has now given all it had to offer and has gone out of fashion. I think that there is some or much truth in these criticisms, depending on the particular case, but they do not reveal the whole truth or even the most important truth about liberation theology. Certainly, they do not reveal the truth of liberation theology as practiced by these Jesuits.

The truth is that liberation theology must advance in all kinds of knowledge, in intellectual self-criticism and in its capacity for systematization. Ignacio Ellacuría frequently stressed this, and he was a thinker of genius who could never be accused of undervaluing the intellectual component of theology. In fact in the UCA we sometimes asked theologians from other countries to help us with the immense capital of theological knowledge they possess, the libraries and time, all of which we lack here. And remember a poignant symbol: the theological library of the

Archbishop Romero Center was partially destroyed after the murders. We are very grateful to the theologians who have assisted us in all this, especially Jesuit and non-Jesuit theologians who have come from Spain to bring us things we lacked, including some of their positive and friendly criticisms, and who also came — as they kept telling us — to learn to do theology in El Salvador.

Having said this, we still need to ask which theology, among the academic and scientific varieties, has captured the essence of scripture and the gospel, God's word today for this moment of history, if we believe that God is still speaking today to creatures? We still have to ask which theology has given a response to humanity's greatest current problem, which is the spoiling of God's own creation through poverty, oppression, and death. We need to ask which theology has made it its business to combine faith and justice, theory and practice, which theology has united theology and spirituality — in the option for the poor. We are fully aware of our limitations and any help or criticism is cordially welcome. But it would be impoverishing and mistaken for academic critics of liberation theology to ignore its novelty and strictly intellectual contribution, its capacity to rediscover absolutely fundamental things about God's revelation, which have slept the sleep of the just for centuries in academic and scientific theologies, its rethinking of the nature of theological knowledge, its reformulation of the concept of verification of theological truths, and the like. Ignacio Ellacuría made an outstanding contribution to this work, insisting that theology should take seriously the signs of the times, so that theology should be the raising of social reality to the status of a theological concept, that theology should be understood as the theory of a historical and ecclesial praxis. (Personally I have reformulated this by saying that theology is *intellectus amoris, misericordiae, iustitiae.*)

There can be honest discussion about whether liberation theology covers many branches of the subject, and it can certainly be asked to systematize these branches better. But I am convinced that it offers us all fundamental knowledge about God and this world, which is really true, serious, reasoned, and well argued, and if you like, scientific. In any case, at least for brother Jesuits who want to do theology, the theology of these Jesuits, liberation theology, shows that it is the most Ignatian theology in the world today, because it is guided by the search for God's will in order to put it into practice and by its following of Jesus today, the Jesus who was poor and lowly.

It is also true, as others say, that liberation theology, as a technically formulated theology, does not reach the majority of ordinary persons, who generally do not even know the name of this theology or of any other. If you like, liberation theology is done by "professionals." But none of this means that it is elitist, pursued by members of an elite in their studies and read by others in their studies too.

Liberation theology is not—directly—a theology for the masses, for the people, any more than any other conventional theology, but it is related very specifically to the lives of the mass of the people because it deals with their real situation, certainly their poverty, their suffering, and hope. Not only that; it also draws on many of the reflections and popular theologies of the communities. Those who do theology about this situation may be few, an elite; but the situation they study is that of many, the poor. Ignacio Ellacuría kept on saying that theology might be done sitting in a study but its starting point was not the study but the poor. The theological truth that is discovered from their viewpoint is returned to them, even though the forms in which it reaches them are not academic, obviously, but little leaflets, sermons, biblical reflections in the communities, song books, and so on. If the mass of ordinary people today understand a little better that what they are suffering is the sin of the world, that God is a God of the poor, their God, that what Jesus proclaimed was a kingdom of life and justice for them, that it was for this that he suffered the fate of the poor and was murdered; if these poor people feel a little more encouraged to work and struggle generously and nobly for life to belong to all, then, even if they have not heard a word of liberation theology, it has still reached them.

Lastly, it is true that liberation theology cannot rest on its laurels. It must address new problems, as it is trying to do: popular religion, the indigenous religions, women, ecology. . . . But what takes my breath away is when people keep saying that liberation theology has gone out of fashion. Of course, it is possible or even probable that this or that book or writer on liberation theology may be going out of date, and as time goes by all of them may gradually become so. But none of this means that liberation theology as such is not—unfortunately—very topical and very urgent, in fact increasingly so. Dom Luciano Mendes de Almeida, the Brazilian Jesuit who is president of the Brazilian bishops' conference, once said, "Liberation theology has put its finger in Latin America's wound." This was true then and it is still true today. Oppression in the Third World is not a fashion, but something very present and increasing. Latin America's wound is not healing but growing bigger and more infected. As Ellacuría repeatedly said, God's creation has not turned out well and it is getting worse. Today there are more millions of poor in the world than yesterday, and fewer than there will be tomorrow.

So it is very important to remember and hold on to the fundamental point: liberation is correlative to oppression, and oppression and injustice are still with us and increasing. Poverty is increasing in the Third World, the gap between the rich and poor countries is widening, there are wars—more than a hundred since the last world war and all of them in the Third World. Cultures are being lost through the imposition of foreign commercial cultures. . . . Oppression is not a fashion. The cries of the oppressed keep rising to heaven and, as Puebla says, more and more loudly. God today goes on hearing these cries, condemning oppression and strengthening liberation. Anyone who does not grasp this, has not understood a word of liberation theology. What I ask myself is what theology is going to do if it ignores this fundamental fact of God's creation as it is. How can a theology call itself "Christian" if it bypasses the crucifixion of whole peoples and their need for resurrection, even though its books have been talking about crucifixion and resurrection for twenty centuries? Therefore if those doing liberation theology are not doing it well, let others do it and do it better. But someone must keep on doing it. And for the love of God, let us not call it a fashion.

Let us hope that the day will come when oppression, demeaning and unjust poverty, cruel and massive repression cease to exist. On that day liberation theology will be obsolete, and this is the day that liberation theologians are working for, even though on that day they will be out of a job. But while oppression lasts—and all statistics show that Latin America is getting poorer—liberation theology is necessary and urgent. It is the only theology that defends the poor of this world—or at least the only one that does so seriously. And let us remember that it is a theology that has martyrs like Ignatius of Antioch and Justin in the early centuries, which, as always, shows that at least it has been a Christian theology.

I do not want what I have been saying to sound abrasive, much less a defense of personal interests, which have little place in my thoughts at the moment. But I do want this to be an appeal for seriousness in theology. The corpses of the Jesuits show that this theology is not elitist but of the people, because it has risen in defense of the people and shared the people's destiny. They show that this theology has said something serious, even scientifically and academically. For let us not forget that what was most feared in these men was their serious and reasoned word, their theological word. They show that oppression—taking the form here of brutal murder—goes on being a horrific reality to which theology must respond. If it does not, it is in vain that it calls itself Christian.

THEIR LEGACY

So what remains? After these reflections, digressions almost, I should like to return, in conclusion, to the fact of the murder itself and ask myself what remains in Salvadoran history and deep in the hearts of us who are still alive. I said at the beginning that for me this murder and martyrdom has been different from all the many others. On other occasions, at the funeral Masses of martyrs, together with the sorrow there was a feeling of hope and even pride and joy in being Christian. This time things have been different and the question that remains has been forced on me in a different form. In this case my answer is very personal, but I hope it will go beyond the personal and say something for everyone.

Above all, the suffering people remain and they have lost some of their protectors. These murders happened in a week of war that left about a thousand dead, countless wounded, many poor houses destroyed and the poor forced to leave their homes and seek refuge elsewhere, as has happened so many times in El Salvador. Others will have the task of political and ethical analysis of the responsibility for what happened, the rightness or wrongness of the FMLN action in the city during these days. And they will have to analyze and judge the reaction of the armed forces. But as always, what is clear is that a people remains who during this week has been even more impoverished, terrorized, and whose hopes of peace have been dissipated yet again.

This is the context in which I see the ultimate malice of the murder of these Jesuits. They have murdered men who defended the poor, and the poor are even more unprotected. And if to these murders are added the persecution campaign during these days against all the churches—something Archbishop Romero condemned—the meaning is very clear: the people are now more helpless. During these days Catholic priests have been murdered, churches full of people seeking refuge have been attacked, Archbishop Rivera and Bishop Rosa Chávez have been threatened and the Salvadoran government even asked John Paul II to remove them from the country. Many members of the Lutheran Church, the Episcopalian Church, and of the Baptist and Mennonite communities have been attacked and captured. Many priests, other Christians, and social workers were threatened with death, in earnest. Bishop Medardo Gomez of the Lutheran Church had to leave the country under diplomatic protection. And of course they have tried to intimidate and muzzle the UCA, the Christian university.

There has been, in other words, an attempt to dismantle the church of the poor, to take from the poor the support and defense these churches offered. Salvadorans know all too well what this means. During the years 1977 to 1980 they tried to dismantle the church in the first big wave of persecution, and we all know what an irreparable loss was suffered in the murder of Archbishop Romero, priests, nuns, catechists, members of base communities. . . . Little by little they have been recovering and now again they are trying to dismantle the church and its defense of the poor. This is the nub of the question and the ultimate malice of these murders: the church is left decimated and the poor even more unprotected. The murder of the six

Jesuits has been first and foremost a great loss for the poor. And as has been said in the past, before the church made an option for the poor, the poor had already made an option for the church, seeking support and hope in it that they could not find anywhere else.

The pain, the doubt, the darkness remain too, and we must not trivialize it. We should not be surprised or ashamed if during these days we feel Job's desolation at God's silence and Jesus' cry on the cross: "My God, my God, why have you forsaken me?" It is not easy to find light and courage in this situation of repression and death, in which the poor are ever more impoverished and weakened. At least for me it has not been easy this time to say from the beginning the true and scandalous words we said on other occasions: "Martyrs are the seed of life"; "Let us give thanks to God for our martyrs." I do not deny the truth of these words, but I did not find it possible to utter them at once, and certainly not as a matter of course.

So what really remains from the martyrdom of these six Jesuits? I believe and hope their spirit remains, that they rise again, like Archbishop Romero, in the Salvadoran people, that they continue to be a light in this dark tunnel, and hope in this country of endless misfortunes. All martyrs rise again in history, each in their own way. Archbishop Romero's is exceptional and unrepeatable, but Rutilio Grande is also present in many peasants, the North American sisters are still alive in Chalatenango and La Libertad, Octavio Ortiz in El Despertar, and the hundreds of martyred peasants in their communities.

The martyred Jesuits too will live on in the Salvadoran people. Fr. Lolo will live on in the Fe y Alegria schools and among the poor who loved him so much for many years. I do not know how the UCA martyrs will rise again. I would like it if the Salvadoran people remembered them as witnesses to the truth, so that they go on believing that the truth is possible in their country; that they remember them as witnesses to justice—structural justice, to put it coldly, or more expressively, love for the people—so that the Salvadoran people retain the courage to believe that it is possible to change the country. I hope they remember them as faithful witnesses to the God of life, so that Salvadorans go on seeing God as their defender; that they remember them as Jesuits who tried to undergo a difficult conversion and paid the price for defending faith and justice. This is what I hope these Jesuits leave the Salvadoran people and that in this legacy they go on being alive, an inspiration and encouragement.

I should like the church, and believers, to remember them as those witnesses to the faith spoken of in the Letter to the Hebrews, and above all, as followers of the witness to *antonomasia*, Jesus, whose life is summed up in Hebrews as compassion to the weak and faithfulness to God. Translated into Jesuit language, may they be remembered as men of justice—the present-day version of mercy—and as men of faith in the God of life in the presence of death—the present-day version of faithfulness. I hope my brothers will stay alive in this legacy.

I hope too that when peace and justice come to the country, succeeding generations remember that these Jesuits were among those who made it possible. I hope that future Christian generations remember their contribution to creating a Salvadoran faith and church, that they are grateful for their witness to the fact that faith and life in El Salvador are not contradictory but empower each other. I hope they recognize that in this way these martyrs guaranteed that faith in Jesus was handed on in El Salvador. I hope, then, that in the future Salvadoran Christians will be grateful to them that the country has attained justice and grown in faith.

The price to be paid for all this has been very high, but inevitable. Today, when so much is said about evangelizing cultures, we should remember a deeper form of evangelization: the evangelization of social life so that society itself becomes good news. And for this to happen it is necessary to become incarnate in that reality, as Archbishop Romero said in words that make us shiver to this day: "I am glad, brothers and sisters, that they have murdered priests in this country, because it would be very sad if in a country where they are murdering the people so horrifically, there were no priests among the victims. It is a sign that the church has become truly incarnate in the problems of the people."

These words, so brutal at first sight, are far-seeing. There can be neither faith nor gospel without incarnation. And with a crucified people, there can be no incarnation without the cross.

Ignacio Ellacuría said many times that the specifically Christian task is to fight to eradicate sin by bearing its burden. This sin brings death, but taking it on, gives credibility. By sharing in the cross of Salvadorans, the church becomes Salvadoran and thus credible. And although in the short term this murder is a great loss, in the long term it is a great gain: we are building a church that is really Christian and really Salvadoran. Christians have shown truly that they are Salvadorans and thus that Salvadorans can really be Christians. This is no small fruit of so much bloodshed in El Salvador, Salvadoran and Christian blood: that faith and justice should walk hand in hand forever.

Finally they leave us a cry to the whole world that does not want to listen, that easily ignores the cries of anonymous peasants, but this cry at least it cannot ignore. This cry is an accusation and a call to conversion. "Blood is the most eloquent of words," said Archbishop Romero. World reaction—even though I do not know whether it will be strong enough to stop the tragedy—have made many think. I am told that even in the U.S. Congress, tough men wept.

They also leave us good news, a gospel. On this sinful and senseless earth it is possible to live like human beings and like Christians. We can share in that current of history that Paul calls life in the Spirit and life in love, in that current of honesty, hope, and commitment that is always being threatened with suffocation but that time and again bursts forth from the depths like a true miracle of God. Joining this current of history, which is that of the poor, has its price, but it encourages us to go on living, working, and believing, it offers meaning and salvation. This is what I believe these new martyrs bequeath us. With it we can go on walking through history, humbly, as the prophet Micah says, amid suffering and darkness, but with God.

In El Salvador today there is much more darkness than light, and the question of hope cannot be answered as a matter of course. In one of the letters I received from El Salvador a great Christian woman wrote to me:

Suddenly it seems that everything has been like a dream and I see all our martyrs going about their daily business. I am not worried about the fathers because I know that they are enjoying our heavenly Father with their robes washed in the blood of martyrdom, but I think about their families and all of us who are still here.

It is not easy to know how to keep on hoping and we must all answer this question in our own way. It seems that everything is against hope, but for me at least, where I see there has been great love, I see hope being born again. This is not a rational conclusion and perhaps not even theological. It is simply true: love produces hope, and great love produces great hope. From Jesus of Nazareth, with many before him and many after him, whenever there has been true love, history has gone on, sinners have been forgiven and offered a future, which, it is hoped, they will accept. Many human beings and Christians have been given that hope. And together with the great love these martyrs had, there are the faces of the poor, in which God is hidden but nevertheless present, asking us to keep going, a request we cannot ignore. The history of sin and grace continues, the history of the poor goes on, and so does the history of God. To keep going amid such darkness is not at all easy, but it is something the poor and the martyrs help us to do so that it becomes possible. It is something we owe the poor and these martyrs.

My six brother Jesuits are at rest now in the Archbishop Romero chapel under a big picture of him. All of them and many others will have given each other a warm embrace and been filled with joy. Our fervent desire is that the heavenly Father send this peace and joy very soon to all Salvadorans. I have written these pages essentially in the hope that the memory of these new martyrs may contribute to peace, justice, dialogue, and reconciliation among all Salvadorans.

Rest in peace Ignacio Ellacuría, Segundo Montes, Ignacio Martín-Baró, Amando López, Juan Ramón Moreno, Joaquin López y López, members of the Society of Jesus, companions of Jesus. Rest in peace Elba and Celina, beloved daughters of God.

May their peace give hope to us who are still alive, and their memory not let us rest in peace.

November 29, 1989
— *Translated by Dinah Livingstone*

PART II

The Martyrs
and
Their Message

$\sim$ 2 $\sim$

Ignacio Ellacuría, S.J.

"Ellacu"
b. Nov. 9, 1930; d. Nov. 16, 1989
Rector, Central American University

The first of the three principal periods of Ellacu's life as a Jesuit, that of his "formation," or education, began with his entrance into the Society of Jesus in 1947 and lasted until he

This and subsequent biographies appeared in a special issue of *Noticias SJ*, the bulletin of the Jesuits' Central American Province (December 1989). They were translated by Thomas Stahel, S.J.

got his Ph.D. in Madrid twenty years later (he was ordained in 1961). One constant during these years was the method of formation he followed for himself—attaching himself to great men, who in his opinion were few. The "greats" were not those of towering intellect, but those who understood and taught in an integrated, convinced, concrete and innovative way, not tied down by rules. Among these greats he always mentioned Miguel Elizondo, who left his mark, as Master of Novices or Tertian Instructor, on five of the six martyred Jesuits. He also cited Karl Rahner, about whom he used to say that Innsbruck wouldn't have been worth the trouble except for him.

When Ellacu arrived in El Salvador for his regency in 1955, there began a period of profound personal development. He began to write for *ECA (Estudios Centroamericanos)* and came to be admired by people outside the Society who heard him speak at one or another lecture. When he went on to Innsbruck in 1958, he once again had to take on the role of student. But the theologate was being buffeted just then by preconciliar winds, and that occasioned Ellacu's first clash with authoritarian "structures." The Spanish speakers used to congregate in his room, and he was so much the leader of the opposition that superiors in Austria were on the point of sending him back to Central America.

A second period of his Jesuit life (1967-75) is that associated with the interior reform of the Society of Jesus going on at that time. Ellacu became the guiding intellect in Central America for this examination of conscience, whose most intense moment and watershed was the Province retreat at San Salvador in December 1969. Ellacu was the organizer and principal speaker, forcefully applying the principles of liberation theology to the Province's situation. Among the archives of the Province one can find the transcripts of these texts, still fresh and brilliant.

Ellacu's leadership was formalized when he was named Delegate for Formation (1971-74). But in 1974, Father Paolo Dezza, one of Father Arrupe's principal assistants, asked that the Provincial superior remove Ellacu as Delegate for Formation. In that same year he also stopped being Province consultor. Ellacu said that is was "back to the trenches" and that he would just dedicate himself to the university.

There, too, he was an innovator. Immediately upon returning from Europe in 1967, he had been named to the board of directors. At that time the university had been in existence for three years, having been conceived as an anti-Marxist alternative to the National University. Its orientation was one of development, both economic and social, for El Salvador. But the arrival of Ellacuría meant that the university took a new turn, toward liberation theology, and it began to conceive of itself as the critical conscience of the country.

The university's new quest for truth and its attendant denunciation of unjust social structures made Ellacu look for a means of communication. The Jesuit Province had the magazine *ECA*, in which he had been writing since 1956. Ellacu and his team caused it to take off in a new direction with a special edition in 1969 on the Salvadoran-Honduran war. They showed that the root of the conflict lay in the unjust landholdings in El Salvador. This was the first issue of a new *ECA*, and, from 1970 on, having passed to the university, the magazine became the principal exponent of the university's critique and Ellacuría's public classroom.

Born in Spain, he became a Salvadoran citizen in 1975. This was necessary to be university rector, and he could see that appointment coming. Moreover, national politics was entering a crisis, and obtaining citizenship would only be more difficult later on.

In that year he also took a political position different from that of certain Jesuit scholastics who would later leave the Society. Ellacu, along with the university, took a public stand distinct from that of groups like the Popular Revolutionary Bloc, and in distancing himself from these, Ellacu also separated himself from young Jesuits who had been dear friends and for whose formation he had fought. So this period ends with Ellacuría getting more and more involved in the university, less and less in intramural Jesuit matters. He was becoming a public personage, and this would lead to his death.

The third and final period of his life (1976-89) is that of Ellacuría the public personality. In 1976 he wrote an editorial in *ECA* strongly criticizing the government for capitulating to the landed oligarchy. This cost the university its national subsidy, and for some months the so-called White Warrior Union set off bombs on the campus. In 1979, Ellacu was named rector (university president, in U.S. terminology), a post he held till his death. After the coup d'etat of that year, a wave of violence swept the country. The university suffered various attacks, including a machine-gunning on the night of February 16, 1980, that left a hundred bullet holes in the Jesuit residence. Archbishop Oscar Romero was assassinated in March.

By 1981, editorials in *ECA* show that Ellacu had come to believe that only a "third way" — a strong societal push for negotiation — could resolve the stalemate between the guerrillas and the government. In October 1985 he became even more important on the public scene as a go-between, along with Archbishop Arturo Rivera y Damas, in the exchange of President Duarte's daughter for 22 political prisoners and 101 wounded guerrillas. This activity gave him greater familiarity with the two contending sides and helped legitimate his call for the way of dialogue.

With the coming to power of Alfredo Cristiani in 1989, Ellacu was hopeful there might be a new impulse toward dialogue on the part of the government. In an *ECA* editorial he distinguished three groups in Cristiani's ARENA party — the Cristiani moderates, the D'Aubuisson militarists, and the secret death-squad capos — and saw the Cristiani line getting stronger. In private, nevertheless, he spoke for the first time since 1982 of the possibility that "it could happen now," by which he meant they might kill him. During the Duarte presidency, when people were anxious and told him to take care, he would say nothing could happen because U.S. policy would not permit it. With ARENA in power, he considered that brake weaker. He did not approve of the guerrilla offensive in November 1989 because he thought it damaged attempts at dialogue.

Ellacu was in the community residence Monday night, November 13, when government soldiers searched it. But he did not sleep there, since he had not yet moved from the old residence. On Tuesday and Wednesday he brought his things over, although he still had not finished moving his books. He did not consider Monday's search a reconnoitering mission, and when someone said it might be, he answered that they should not be paranoid. Since the soldiers had seen they didn't have anything, that would be the end of it. Besides, if they went into hiding, that could be interpreted as a sign they had done something wrong.

How could someone so intelligent have been so mistaken? Many have wondered about that. When people would ask Ellacu if he were not afraid, he would say no, but, he added, he no more took credit for that than for lacking a sense of smell. He just didn't have one.

His last theology article contains the following sentence, much quoted nowadays as prophetic: "The Spirit breathes in many ways, and supreme among them is the disposition to give one's life for others, whether by tireless daily commitment or by the sacrifice of a violent death."

Persecution for the Sake of the Reign of God

The true people of God in a world dominated by sin cannot but be persecuted, because as people of God it seeks to negate sin and to establish a Reign that to a great extent is the negation of existing structures. That is what Jesus proclaimed, and he made persecution a clear sign of the happiness that comes with belonging to God's Reign. Hence Archbishop Romero would say:

> Christ encourages us not to fear persecution, because, believe me, brothers and sisters, one who is committed to the poor must encounter the same fate as the poor. And in El Salvador we already know what the fate of the poor means: to disappear, be tortured and abducted, with bodies showing up.
>
> I rejoice, brothers and sisters, that our church is persecuted precisely for its preferential option for the poor and for trying to be incarnate on behalf of the poor.
>
> It would be sad if in a country where people are being murdered so frightfully, we would not find priests among the victims as well. They give witness to a church incarnate in the problems of the people.
>
> My only consolation is that Christ, who wanted to com-

This is the conclusion to an essay, "El Verdadero Pueblo de Dios, Segun Mons. Romero," that appeared in Ignacio Ellacuría's book, *Conversión de la Iglesia al Reino de Dios: Para anunciarlo y realizarlo en la historia* (Santander, Spain: Editorial Sal Terrae, 1984). The essay outlines the characteristics of the church, or "the true people of God," as reflected in the witness of Archbishop Romero. Aside from the mark of persecution, Ellacuría refers to the preferential option for the poor, the incarnation in the historical struggles of the people for justice and liberation, and the introduction of a Christian leaven in the struggle for justice. Those themes are also recapitulated in the section reprinted here. The translation is by Phillip Berryman.

municate this great truth, also encountered incomprehension and they called him a rabble-rouser and condemned him to death, as they have threatened me these days.

I want to assure you, and I ask you to pray that I be faithful to this promise, that I will not abandon my people, but along with the people I will share all the risks that my ministry demands.

Do not keep silencing with violence those of us who are extending this invitation. And do not keep on killing those of us who are trying to bring about a more just distribution of power and wealth in our country. I speak in the first person because this week I received a warning that I am on the list of those who are going to be eliminated next week. But let it be clear that no one can kill the voice of justice any more.

I have often been threatened with death. I must tell you that as a Christian I do not believe in death without resurrection. If they kill me, I will rise in the Salvadoran people. I say that with no boasting, but with the greatest humility. . . .

As pastor, I am obliged by divine orders to give my life for those whom I love, and that means all Salvadorans, even for those who might kill me. If the threats are carried out, as of now I offer my blood to God for the redemption and resurrection of El Salvador. . . . Martyrdom is a grace I do not think I deserve. But if God accepts the sacrifice of my life, may my blood be the seed of freedom and the sign that hope will soon be a reality. . . . May my death, if it is accepted by God, be for the liberation of my people and as a witness of hope in the future. . . . Better, of course, that they realize that they will be wasting their time. A bishop will die, but God's church, which is the people, will never perish.[1]

These quotes bring together Archbishop Romero's witness on the historic necessity, in accordance with what Jesus said, that the people of God be persecuted when it follows in Jesus' steps. They also evidence his growing belief that his life would be taken by those who could not stand the fact that he had so effectively become the voice of those who had been robbed even of their words.

He saw persecution as an inevitable consequence of commitment to the poor, and he was well aware of the fate of the poor who were struggling for their liberation or of those whom the oppressors regarded as potential candidates for that struggle. The preferential option for the poor, an active option, is what brings persecution on the church; being incarnate among the poor is what brings on the church in El Salvador all kinds of persecution, from calumny and harassment to exile and death. It is obvious that a good part of the church in El Salvador has committed itself fully to defending the cause of the poor, not in an abstract or general way, but by fighting the abuses of repression, and encouraging those who are struggling together for their rights. The response has not been slow in coming: one bishop dead, ten priests murdered; three sisters and a lay missioner raped, tortured, and murdered; dozens of preachers of the word disappeared, tortured, and then slaughtered; dozens of priests and religious in exile; churches, schools, and residences assaulted, searched, shot up; church publications and media dynamited. . . . In the annals of ecclesial life today, it is hard to find a church as martyred and persecuted simply for being faithful to its commitment to the poor, and for striving to be the true people of God.

The cowardly, the "prudent," and those with interests to protect say that all this is happening to the church for getting involved in politics. But Archbishop Romero asked himself: Would Jesus have taken any other course? For the same accusation was leveled at Jesus: "We found this man subverting our nation" (Luke 23:2), stirring things up from Galilee to Judea, and risking repressive intervention by the Romans. If politics is understood to mean incarnating the gospel message in the processes of history and encouraging popular struggles in what is just about them, the church of El Salvador has gotten into politics; if politics is understood to mean denouncing oppressors and those who do violence to the people, calling sin sin and grace grace, then the church has been involved in politics. It has not been persecuted for defending dogmas, which for the moment do not bother those who wield power in this world; but it has been persecuted for heroically incarnating Christian virtues, and especially for standing with the poor and the persecuted.

The church in El Salvador has not protested over limitations placed on its institutional rights or privileges; it has not been persecuted for actions in defense of its interests (and in fact it has not taken such actions); it has been persecuted for defending the rights and interests of the poor, for attacking the selfishness and greed of the rich, and the outrages of the military. Archbishop Romero and his church defended the poor; they judged political developments from the standpoint of the history of the reign of God. They did that even against the popular organizations, when they did not pay enough attention to the real values of the people or when they proposed solutions but then carried out actions that were not in harmony with the most adequate way of embodying the Reign of God. In those instances, however, the popular forces did not respond by persecuting the church. They have not even done so toward those elements that have identified with the government, the military, and the dominant structures. That difference alone would be enough for assessing who is who, and what constitutes true persecution of the true people of God.

With regard to personal persecution of Archbishop Romero culminating in his murder before the altar of God, as he was about to begin the eucharistic sacrifice, one feels in the premonitions cited above an echo of the premonitions of Jesus—written *post eventum*—when facing his imminent passion. In the very sequence of dates, there is evidence as his statements become more urgent. What alarmed him was the overall situation, which was deteriorating more and more. He felt that they were calling him a rabble-rouser as they had Jesus and they were condemning him in the same way, but that did not keep him from going up to his Jerusalem, nor did he stop carrying out any of his normal pastoral duties. Romero went along in Lent toward Calvary but did not even get to Palm Sunday—that day he went into his cathedral and entered the sanctuary in episcopal vestments, but now carried on priests' shoulders, and lying in a casket. As everyone knows, he could not even be buried in peace. His people were again slaughtered and his body had to be buried in haste. Not even then did he abandon his people nor did his people abandon him; neither did his persecutors and detractors, who wanted to keep the people from emerging from the martyrdom of their pastor with hope; they wanted to plunge his people deeper into death in order to stifle their hope that resurrection would come soon. But he had left his voice and his presence still alive: "Let it be clear that no one can kill the voice of justice any more"; "If they kill me, I will rise in the Salvadoran people"; "A bishop will die, but the church of God, which is the people, will never perish."

This combination of the people being persecuted and Archbishop Romero being persecuted provides a preeminent example of what is happening in this chain of persecutions. First of all there is the persecution of the people, a persecution that at its root is that of structural oppression and then becomes repression when the people have become conscious and have organized struggles for liberation. Then comes the persecution of the people of God, which seeks to bring salvation history into the history of the people and to integrate the history of the people into salvation history. Finally, there is the persecution and death of Archbishop Romero, as the most visible head of the people of God, whose death it is hoped will scatter the flock. That has not happened completely, but the enemy of the people and of the Reign of God in history was well aware that it was going to be difficult to replace a prophet and a bishop like Archbishop Romero. For it is the same ones who murder the people who killed him, and they did so with the same impunity with which they kill the people. He was not a North American, for whom the CIA and FBI might swing into action to discover his murderers, and the Salvadoran authorites "cannot" do so, despite their repeated futile promises to investigate exhaustively. They cannot investigate and they do not want to do so, and there is no one to demand that they do so, as the church and the people of the United States demand of U.S. authorities, with results that are both effective and revealing.

The political significance and the theological significance of this death and these persecutions is thus clear. From a theological standpoint, the death of the prophet results from preaching the Reign of God with words involved in history, words that arouse movements in history; politically speaking, the death of the religious leader is intended to halt the popular movement and the church's support for that movement. The same is to be said of the persecution of the people of God: its action against structures and forces that are the embodiment of sin is an action against sin and against the prevailing structures and forces, and it is one more threat to its age-old domination and exploitation.

Something different should be said about persecution of the people, which seeks to take from the dominant class and its faithful servants the power to dominate and exploit. In this case, action is directly political, although indirectly and implicitly it may also be an action on behalf of God's Reign.

But there may be confluence between those who begin from the earthly character of the struggle against injustice and those whose starting point is the Christian character of bringing about the Reign. The two paths are different, but they may be connected objectively even if it is not recognized subjectively. If it has been said that true Christian faith must be linked to the promotion of justice, it would not be an exaggeration to state that there must also be a connection between the promotion of justice and Christian faith. The touchstone of one and the same persecution can serve as a criterion for gradually connecting things that may at first seem disconnected. The reality of action may be a more solid foundation than any ideological formulation.

The problem is not easy, either in theory or in practice. Even though it be carried out by Marxists, practice is an area of confluence with Christian faith from the standpoint of the Reign of God. Not to see it that way is to politicize the question too much on the side of those Christians who do not want to see, and to ideologize it too much on the side of Marxists who likewise do not want to see. And the truth should weigh more than politics and ideology.

These are some of the characteristics of the true people of God, as viewed from the present situation of the Salvadoran people and from the inexhaustible example of Archbishop Romero. Others can be noted. Indeed, those noted here imply others, and necessarily spread out into many more. They are like the string of a much larger mass of wool, but perhaps they are like the one string that has to be pulled so that the yarn will not get tangled and may be useful for weaving the life of the church and the life of the people. This is not reductionism, but simply seeking the true path to the true totality. Here the words of Archbishop Romero on another topic are applicable: "I believe the bishop always has a great deal to learn from the people. And it is precisely in the charisms that the Spirit gives the people that the bishop finds the touchstone of his authenticity."[2] These characteristics of the people of God that we have noted here, because they are both needs of the people and pressing demands of faith, are thereby also the touchstone of the authenticity of the people of God, to which bishops should pay much more attention than they do. In the church the people of God is much more important than the church's institutional aspects, its human ways of being constituted as a society. Bishops and faithful, however, are often much more concerned about those institutional aspects than about the life of God's people.

None of this goes against the church's hierarchical character, although that is the great fear of those who occupy positions of authority. No one seriously questioned Archbishop Romero's hierarchical authority, but he exercised it not as the powers of this world, who delight in adulation and seek to wield authority, but as Jesus exercised authority with his disciples, and as he through word and example ordered that it be exercised. The institutional church, at least in its spirit, should shape itself like that first base community made up of Jesus and his followers and disciples; base communities should not be made to take shape along the lines of an established church, which in much of its behavior has become worldly. First came the base community as the initial cell of the people of God seeking the Reign, and it was from that point that the church gradually emerged. Although we cannot develop this point now, this hint may be helpful for resolving the argument of whether or not Jesus directly and expressly founded a church.

Thus we see the people giving the church its authenticity, for in the people the power of the spirit and the truth of the Son, who has emptied himself, are at work, and we see the church continually communicating life and salvation to the people. "Today our people are very well prepared, and everything around them is preaching the cross to us; but those who have faith and Christian hope know that behind this Calvary of El Salvador stands our passover, our resurrection, and that is the hope of the Christian people," said Archbishop Romero on the eve of his death.[3] "That is why, as all week long I go my way gathering up the cry of the people and their suffering from so much crime, and from the ignominy of so much violence, I pray the Lord to give me the right words for consoling, for denouncing, for calling to repentance. And although I continue to be a voice crying in the desert, I know that the church is making the effort to carry out its mission."[4] What God wants is to make the history of peoples a history of salvation, but for that purpose through the preferential way of the poor God plunges into this history of peoples those who have been first called to be the permanent core of the people of God.

For those who suspect that behind this whole formulation there is a flight from personal responsibility and individual conversion, it is well to recall Archbishop Romero's words:

> How easy it is to denounce structural injustice, institutionalized violence, social sin! All that is true, but where are the roots of social sin? In the heart of each human being. Present-day society is like some kind of limited corporation: no one wants to accept the blame of all who are responsible. We are all sinners and we have all contributed our bit to the huge accumulation of crimes and violence in our country. . . . Thus salvation begins with the human being, with the dignity of the human being, uprooting the sin in each human being.[5]

Today in our situation the authenticity of the people of God goes by way of poverty and justice: they are the touchstone of the truth of the faith that is professed and of the genuineness of life as it is lived out: poverty, which involves incarnating all our efforts and incarnating ourselves in the reality of the oppressed majorities, and that will necessarily entail a voluntary impoverishment and abnegation on the part of those who wield power; justice, which involves giving to the people what belongs to the people and struggling to uproot injustice and exploitation, and to establish a new earth, wherein the life of the new human may be possible. Such a human being has already been made new in poverty and justice, through the destruction of the old order, but there is still much to be done to complete this newness in the building of a new order, where the causes of social exploitation and individual oppression will disappear to the greatest extent possible.

I should like to finish this subject by returning to the quote, "those who once were not even a people and are now people of God." This deep idea from the First Letter of Peter, with profound echoes of the prophets, connects two distinct realities: people and people of God. I do not intend to analyze the text exegetically, but rather to make a theological projection relevant to the situation of the Salvadoran people, and hence to the situation of numerous other peoples at different points in their struggle for liberation.

The predicament of many of these peoples is that they are not yet even a people. The point is not that they are not a people in a sociological or political sense, especially when viewed in merely formal terms, but that they are not a people in reality: they are not, because years of underdevelopment, exploitation, oppression, and repression have prevented them from being what they should be, from growing and developing as they should, and from giving the best they have; they are not, because they have been blocked from enjoying their own land and the labor of their own hands; they are not, because they have been deprived of being forgers of their own destiny and from participating in the economic, social, and political power that should be theirs; they are not, because they have not even been permitted to enjoy their own culture and to express creatively what they have inside themselves. The result is that a good part of the people strives for survival along mistaken paths: machismo, getting even, contempt for life, selfish antagonisms, violence. ... There is no reason to idealize the people, either in the individuals and groups that make it up or as a whole body. The greatness of the people lies beneath these weaknesses and beyond these failings; its greatness lies in the fact that God has chosen it, just as it is, to overturn the mighty from their thrones, for in this same people, the people of the poor and the oppressed, there are great virtues of solidarity, sacrifice, hope, and openness.

In the case of El Salvador, this people has within it magnificent religious values and magnificent Christian virtues. It is very receptive to the Christian message when it is directed at its problems, its expectations, and its complaints. Thus Archbishop Romero, who talked simultaneously of the history of God and the history of the people, found such a great reception among the people, a reception incomparably beyond that of any other bishop or any other political leader. Out of his people he drew the question, which was already an initial response, and illuminated by the gospel, he returned it enriched and enflamed. He was unquestionably their pastor, the one who really knew them and the one they really knew. "With this people it is not hard to be a good shepherd. This people presses into its service those of us who have been called to defend their rights and be their voice."[6]

And with God's word, with God's life, with faith in Jesus Christ, with the hope of the Reign, Archbishop Romero wanted to make this people a people, and a people of God. He was convinced that if it did not become people of God—worse, if it was prevented from being people of God—it would never truly become a people. That is why he cried out against those who were preventing it from being a people, but he also protested against those who feared that the people might continue to be, or might become, a people of God. That was also not respecting the people, that was also failing to understand what a genuine preaching of the Christian message can do for a people, improving its morale, encouraging its spirit, humanizing its suffering and its victories, tempering its political projects, purifying its personal behavior. A revolution unable to respect the people's faith, and incapable of acknowledging the contribution of Christian faith to the awakening of the Salvadoran collective consciousness, would be quite inadequate.

The same can be said of the popular organizations. Archbishop Romero and Bishop Rivera were so encouraging to those organizations in their joint pastoral letter, which the other four Salvadoran bishops found incomprehensible. They gave encouragement to those organizations, but they also criticized them, when in the name of frozen dogmatism and issues from the past, they might jeopardize the faith of organization members, who out of their faith opted for revolutionary struggle. Not only does faith not necessarily conflict with revolution and the true interests of the people, it can even be one of its safeguards and supports.

But that requires that there be a pastoral practice of accompaniment, as Archbishop Romero advocated in his last pastoral letter.[7] This entails entering in a priestly and missionary way into the people as it is struggling and becoming organized. Perhaps on this point there have been serious faults on both sides. For their part, the organizations may be afraid that the free word of the priest or delegate of the word might become a point of independence and of criticism within a structure that is intended to be monolithic and disciplined, or perhaps because what they expect from Christians is not their explicitly Christian contribution, but their political contribution.

Unquestionably there have been efforts to utilize the faith, because a problem has been seen in a short-range and prejudiced way, thus stifling the fruitfulness of the faith. But the time for mistrust should be gone and the time should come for recognizing how necessary it is that the Christian spirit provide more and more inspiration for the cause of the people. For its part, the church may have been afraid of the revolutionary struggle on the easy pretext that it was Marxist and the comfortable excuse that the church was being used. Why cannot the church see that the closer it gets and the deeper it goes into these struggles and the revolutionary process the more it will be able to influence them, and the more it will be able to impregnate them with gospel values, and even with the true Christian faith? This cannot be done from outside, by warning of dangers, condemning actions that are not understood, offering bits of advice that are useless because there is no moral authority behind them. It must be done from within, for how are they going to believe if they have not heard the word? And how are they going to hear the word if it is not proclaimed to them? And how is it going to be proclaimed to them if no one is sent to them, if it is a word sent in from outside?

We cannot build up the people of God with our backs to the

people, to the vast and exploited popular majorities, and to their real problems and struggles. ... The presence of God in the people, in their suffering and joy, in their defeats and victories, cannot but benefit the people, if it is a liberating God who presses toward a better future, in which everything will be new: the heavens, the earth, and human beings themselves. Few cases exemplify as marvelously as that of Archbishop Romero how to unite the interests of the people to God's interests, history to transcendence, the fallen to the elevated human being, and the people to the true people of God.

NOTES

1. Sermons of Archbishop Romero: February 17, 1980; July 15, 1979; June 24, 1979; June 3, 1979; November 11, 1979; February 24, 1980 (last two passages).

2. Sermon, September 9, 1979.

3. Sermon, March 23, 1980.

4. Ibid.

5. Ibid.

6. Sermon, November 18, 1979.

7. Fourth pastoral letter in Archbishop Oscar Romero, *Voice of the Voiceless* (Maryknoll, N.Y.: Orbis Books, 1985), pp. 114–161.

~ 3 ~

Ignacio Martín-Baró, S.J.

"Nacho"
b. Nov. 7, 1942; d. Nov. 16, 1989
Vice Rector of the University

As a young Jesuit, "Nacho" was very observant and disciplined, even somewhat rigid and unyielding, one of those who adhered to the letter of the law. Some of his classmates were not at ease with such perfectionism, but once they got to know him and like him, they worked at "humanizing" him, to the point that Nacho, boon companion that he became, was the one who would be sent to ask superiors for tough permissions. And at

76

parties, he would sing with the guitar and relax, laying aside his mantle of seriousness.

In fact, Nacho seemed to be two people: the one who was strict with students and worked too hard (16 hours a day), intense and mysterious, sometimes neglecting to return a greeting; and the one who was amiable, considerate in a thousand ways with secretaries, students and campesinos, the one who always enjoyed birthday parties, the beloved pastor of Jayaque. These two Nachos were one and the same, or so it seemed to those who were closest to him. Ten days before his death he was celebrating his own birthday and announced aloud his plans to relax his pace — "Celebrations help release tension."

As everyone knows, Nacho was not only super-gifted but multi-gifted. Nevertheless, he concentrated his interests. From the time of his philosophy studies in Colombia, he pursued the study of psychology, devouring books on his own. He continued studying and teaching psychology at the university in San Salvador after he was ordained a priest. Given his talent and the need he felt for further training in theory and method, he was sent to the University of Chicago, where he got his doctorate in three years (1979). This professional preparation meant that his research and publications then took off, gaining international recognition for their quality and rigor.

Administrative tasks bored him, and he often said in the last few months that he was going to resign as academic vice rector. Research is what attracted him, and he felt fulfilled when he sat down to work at his computer. He wrote for many journals, and when they asked him for scholarly contributions, he would tell them they had to wait, because he always had six or seven articles in the works. In this, as in other things, he was so obliging that it cost him to turn anyone down. He joked that he was like a prostitute who said yes to everybody.

His interest in personal psychology, and especially among the poor, was not just bookish. Once a young girl tried to kill herself in the street next to his office. He gave her medical attention, counseled her and told her to come back and see him when she was released from the hospital. After listening to her whole story, he took her to a cafeteria, gave her some money, then got her a job and a place to stay. After his funeral, she said: "I never believed such goodness existed," and, tearfully, "Why didn't I die instead of him?"

The university was his base of operations for the weekly trips to Jayaque, a campesino community surrounded by coffee plantations. He begged rolls of film so he could give photos to the campesinos. Looking for a statue of the Virgin to put in a country chapel, he even went to the cemetery where they made such statues from cement. He bought the children candies and always carried some with him. Nacho was accustomed to give interviews to foreign journalists according to set appointments, but whenever his campesinos came from Jayaque, they entered his office without waiting.

He did this pastoral work in Jayaque with a team of sisters and a group of younger Jesuits, some of whom were priests, but for the sisters he was always "the" priest. The campesinos, too, accorded him special respect. He said Mass in the town and outlying districts, took part in their parish meetings (always according to plan), was on hand for cursillos and fiestas. The younger Jesuits, who at the university regarded him as severe, saw him here in a new light.

Nacho died next to Ellacuría. They were always complements to each other. Ellacuría did social analysis to draw from it a policy that he might then put in practice. Nacho, on the other hand, as an outstanding social scientist of rather more empirical cut, offered data from which the public might draw its own conclusions. He had a religious passion for the poor and for justice, but his writings were calmer. At the moment of death, however, it was Nacho's voice that was the strongest. His was the only one that the witness heard, shouting at the soldiers: "This is unjust! You're rotten!"

Political Violence and War as Causes of
Psychosocial Trauma in El Salvador

TWO IMAGES OF EL SALVADOR

According to an image widely circulated by U.S. government spokespersons, El Salvador represents the best example of the "new Latin American democracies" that have emerged during the last decade, particularly in the Central American region, with the exception of Nicaragua. In support of this statement, the following points are made:

1. The Salvadoran government was chosen in free elections, in accordance with a democratic constitution.

2. There is a growing respect for human rights among the country's population. According to the U.S. government, 80 percent of the human rights violations that still occur are committed by the rebels.

3. The Salvadoran army has become increasingly professional and submits to civilian control.

4. Although there are still a few problems, for example, in the functioning of the judicial system, to a large extent this should be attributed to the situation created by the Marxist-Leninist groups practicing violent terrorism with support from Cuba and Nicaragua.

Regrettably, this image of the country reflects little, if anything, of the real situation of El Salvador. The democratic character of a government does not depend — at least not solely — on the way in which it is elected, but rather on the forces that determine its day-to-day conduct. And the verifiable fact is that, in terms of El Salvador's basic policies, North American fears about "national security" count more than the most basic needs

---

This article first appeared in 1988 in the *International Journal of Mental Health* vol. 18, no. 1, pp. 3-20. It is reprinted with permission of the publisher, M.E. Sharpe, Inc.

of the Salvadoran people. It would never cross any Salvadoran's mind that the Duarte government might have some significant control over the Salvadoran armed forces: this is simply a result of the daily experience Salvadorans have of who is in charge there. And in the end, attributing the majority of human rights violations to the rebels does not exempt the government from its share of the responsibility. Moreover, the fact is that such attribution constitutes a gross distortion of the evidence, as has been made clear by independent observers.[1]

What, then, is the reality of El Salvador? Instead of making "generic" statements, a series of facts of daily life will be presented that directly relate to mental health and reveal a Salvadoran reality very different from that depicted above:

> Let us consider a small community in the Department of Chalatenango, in the northern part of the country. This is one of the most conflictive zones, effectively controlled by insurgents of the FMLN (Farabundo Marti National Liberation Front) for a good part of the year. The residents consist of a few dozen very poor campesino families: the elderly, a few adult men, women, and children; there are no youths.
>
> Periodically the army launches military operations affecting this small village, including the destruction of homes and crops. Every time an operation is begun, the people take shelter in their houses gripped by a series of psychosomatic symptoms: generalized trembling of the body, muscular weakness, diarrhea. . . . One elderly couple has chosen, since the beginning of the war, to hide in a *tatu*, or shelter, every time there is an operation or when the armed forces approach the area. The result has been that the mere announcement that there will be an operation produces in the husband what the whole village calls "the pain": violent intestinal cramps, a crushing headache, and a generalized weakness that makes it impossible to walk.

A small study carried out in 1987 in the refuge of San José Calle Real, situated on the outskirts of San Salvador, among 250 people of all ages (36 percent of the refugees there), found that the presence of the army in the vicinity of the refuge was sufficient to cause 87 percent of those questioned to experience fear; 75 percent felt an accelerated pulse rate, and 64 percent were overcome by generalized bodily trembling:

> Usulután is an area in the southeast part of the country with two different regions: a coastal zone, rich in cotton production, and a more mountainous zone, with large coffee farms. In this area there is a permanent presence of the FMLN, and the armed forces carry out continuous counterinsurgency operations.
>
> In the course of a series of opinion polls, we have gathered clear evidence that government soldiers practice systematic sexual abuse of the campesina women living in the area. One of these women told us that in order to avoid the continuing mass rape, the "cleverest ones" (*las más listas* was the expression she used) resort to the protection of some soldier or official, prostituting themselves to him so that he will protect them from the other soldiers. According to our information, this is a common practice among the members of the government armed forces, but not among members of the FMLN.[2]

In an opinion poll conducted in February 1988, campesinos were asked to indicate what they considered to be the causes of the war. Of those interviewed, who had expressed themselves very freely up until that moment, 59.1 percent appeared frightened and answered that they did not know anything about it. Even when they were shown obvious results of the war—burnt crops, the marks of bullets or bombs on their own houses—they insisted on their ignorance, saying that these things had happened when they were not home. It is clear that although fear may have diminished in recent years among the population in the urban area of San Salvador, it continues to be very prevalent among the campesinos, including those who live in less-conflictive areas of the country:

> There is an increasing number of massacres of civilians by soldiers on leave or by former soldiers, who throw grenades

at a home, into a bus, or in the middle of a dance hall. Often those who commit these acts are found to have been drunk. The motives tend to be jealousy or the desire to assert their power or "authority." In just the last week of February 1988, the press reported no fewer that four such cases.

In a research project carried out between April and May of 1987, we tried to replicate some North American studies on the formation of the concept of social class.[3] More than two hundred children of various ages, belonging to various social sectors, were interviewed. One of the questions asked was: "What would have to happen in order for there to be no poor people?" Several of the children from the higher socioeconomic sectors gave this response: "Kill them all."

Of course, this piece of data can be interpreted in various ways, and the study is still unfinished. But the studies carried out in the United States have never reported this kind of answer. It should be added that some sectors of Salvadoran society propose as a solution to the civil war the elimination of "all the subversives," in the style of the 1932 mass killing that took place in the country[4] in order to "win in this way another fifty years of peace."

These four examples present an image of El Salvador that is very different from that offered in official reports. Moreover, they point to a social and political framework without which it is impossible to understand the problems of both the Salvadorans who stay in the country and of those who seek refuge abroad. Three features can be useful in defining that reality.

1. Above all, this is a society that is more than poor—it is impoverished; a society that is not just divided—it is violently torn apart. It is a society in which the most basic human rights of the majority are structurally and systematically denied—such fundamental rights as having a place to live, a job in which to fulfill oneself as a human being, or a school in which to educate one's children.[5] This situation demonstrates how arbitrary and deceptive it can be to distinguish between "economic" and "political" refugees: in El Salvador to demand the satisfaction

of the basic needs of the poor majority is, in itself, a "subversive" proposition since it attacks the very bases of a discriminatory system.

2. The government's armed forces continue to represent, for the majority of Salvadorans, a terrifying and abusive force, arbitrary and omnipotent "authority," and the expression of a system organized to serve the needs of a minority of 10 percent or 15 percent of the population. This is not meant to deny the partial improvements since 1984 in the Salvadoran army, in both its technical performance and in its relations with the civilian population. Nevertheless, the armed forces in El Salvador continue to be an institution beyond the law. Whether or not its members respect human rights depends on the discretion of its collective interests and, worse, on the generally narrow understanding the local officials or common soldiers ("the authorities") bring to each situation.

3. The Salvadoran population is being systematically destroyed by the war, which has devastated the country for eight years, and which the U.S. military advisers calculate may continue for another eight years. Obviously, a very fundamental part of this destruction is the number of victims: the death toll from the conflict during these last few years is estimated to amount to nearly seventy thousand.[6] It is difficult to give an exact number for the wounded, though it is known that in military combat in general there are at least three wounded for each fatality.

But what I am interested in emphasizing here is not so much the physical destruction as the psychosocial destruction. As illustrated above, the impact of the Salvadoran war ranges from the kind of organic deterioration manifested in psychosomatic symptoms, to the aberrant criminalization of children's minds, to the unhinging of social relations as they are submitted to the abuse and violence of those who hold power in their hands.

THE SALVADORAN WAR

All wars constitute a way of resolving conflict between groups; it is characterized by a resort to violence in an attempt to destroy or dominate one's rival. Psychological studies on war tend to concentrate predominantly on two areas. One seeks to improve the efficiency of military actions by focusing on those very elements that contribute to the war effort (what is called "psychological warfare"); the other concentrates on the psychological consequences of the war, and is oriented toward prevention and treatment.

There is, nevertheless, an aspect of war that is of great importance and should be analyzed by social psychology: its way of defining all that is social. By its very dynamic, a war tends to become the most all-encompassing phenomenon of a country's situation, the dominant process to which all other social, economic, political, and cultural processes must be subordinated, and which, directly or indirectly, affects all the members of a society.

But this same absorbing quality of the war can lead to ignoring the different ways in which it affects groups and individuals: what represents ruin for some becomes big business for others, and what places some close to death opens for others the possibility of a new life. The war suffered in the flesh by the campesino is one thing; what the urban middle class contemplates on the television screen is quite another. In El Salvador, those who go to the battlefields are generally the poor, the children of campesinos or the urban poor, not the children of the factory owner or the professional.

From a psychosocial perspective, the Salvadoran civil war was marked in 1984 by three fundamental characteristics: (1) violence, which directs the best resources of each contestant toward the destruction of its rival; (2) social polarization—that is, the displacement of groups toward opposite extremes, with a resultant rigidification of their respective ideological positions and pressure exerted upon everyone to align himself or herself with "us" or "them"; and (3) the institutional lie, involving such effects as distortion of institutions' purposes and ideological screening of social reality.[7]

Fundamentally, this psychosocial characterization of the Salvadoran war continued to hold true in 1988. But the fact that the situation of the war still has not substantially changed in spite of the blood spilled, the hundreds of millions of dollars invested by the United States, the destruction and the suffering, is an indication that either the war is not the solution to the conflict or that it is wrongly conducted.[8] All in all, it seems necessary to examine the variations that the three psychosocial characteristics of the Salvadoran civil war have assumed as the war drags on if Axis IV of DSM-III[9] concerning situational and psychosocial precipitants of mental problems is to be taken seriously.

Social Polarization

In 1984 the degree of polarization of the Salvadoran population seemed to have reached a peak, and significant signs of depolarization could be observed—that is, conscious efforts by some groups and sectors to dissociate themselves from either side.[10] The processes of polarization and depolarization are neither uniform nor mechanical. Instead, they are closely related to the progress of military activity and to the evolution of the political situation itself. In this sense, from 1984 until the present, various important processes have been observable. Perhaps the most significant is the resurgence of mass movements, with clear sympathies toward the position of the FMLN.

Nevertheless, the conscious effort to polarize and take the grassroots organizations beyond labor demands toward more conscious political, radical, and even violent positions has produced a new reduction in the movement. Some have drawn away who feel they lack the strength to enter into this dynamic, or who fear a repetition of the violent repression of 1981–1982. On the governmental side, the armed forces have embarked on many plans of counterinsurgency, one of whose essential ingredients is the so-called psychological war. These plans have expressly sought to win "the hearts and minds" of the civilian population, to create a major obstacle for the rebels by presenting them as common terrorists and enemies of the people. A concerted effort has been made not only to maintain the social polarization but to extend and deepen it. Toward this end, both sides have tried to emphasize points of antagonism rather than points of possible agreement, exploiting sources of resentment and of intergroup hatred. Each group has presented the other as the incarnation of evil, as "the enemy" that must be eliminated. Government propaganda is more contradictory in this aspect than the propaganda of the FMLN, owing as much to its volume and intensity (incomparably greater) as to its distortion of language.

The degree of social polarization currently in the country is probably less than it was during the first years of the civil war. Bad as the situation may be, some political spaces have been opening, whether because of weariness and reason, disillusionment with a military solution and the daily demands of getting along, or international pressure and the emergence of various options. Some people are attempting to take advantage of these spaces to build bridges and to map out new horizons. The "National Debate" launched by the Catholic Church in August 1988, which assembled sixty significant social groups (unions, universities, professional associations, and others) and reached fundamental agreements about how to end the war, has been the best example of efforts toward social reconciliation.[11]

Certainly, the amount of resources required to maintain the social polarization gives an indication of the Salvadoran people's growing resistance to the attempt to solve the conflict by military means. However, the results of this resistance are not entirely positive, since the resistance can take such forms as inhibition or skepticism, which are not necessarily socially or personally constructive.

But even though the level of social polarization has tended to diminish and a popular resistance is developing that is deaf to all efforts to further radicalize the conflict, the campaigns of polarization keep the country in an atmosphere of tension. This tension is not just military but psychosocial as well: facts are ideologized, people are demonized, and the use of those very political spaces that have begun to open is criminalized—all of which leads to an apparent stagnation of social confrontation and to greater difficulty in trying to establish spaces for interaction of the various social groups with respect to objectives they share.

The Institutionalized Lie

The systematic screening of reality continues to be one of the fundamental characteristics of the Salvadoran war. This screening assumes various forms:

1. Above all, the object is to create an official version of the

facts, an "official story," which ignores crucial aspects of reality, distorts others, and even falsifies or invents still others. This official story is imposed by means of an intense and extremely aggressive display of propaganda, which is backed up even by all the weight of the highest official positions. Thus, for example, the president of the country became the public guarantor of an official explanation that attempted to blame the FMLN for the murder of the president of the Nongovernmental Commission of Human Rights, Herbert Anaya Sanabria.

2. When, for whatever reason, facts come to light that directly contradict the "official story," they are "cordoned off." A circle of silence is imposed that relegates the facts to quick oblivion or to a past that is presumably superseded by the evolution of events. The continual violations of human rights by members of the armed forces enter this realm of blanketing silence.

3. Public statements about the national reality, the reporting of violations of human rights, and, above all, the unmasking of the official story, of the institutionalized lie, are considered "subversive" activities — in fact they are, since they subvert the order of the established lie. Thus, we come to the paradox that whoever dares to state the reality or to report abuses becomes, by this very act, a culprit of justice. What seems to be important is not whether the facts in question are true or not, which is always denied a priori; what is important is that they are stated. It is not the deeds that count, but the images.

For example, when the auxiliary bishop of San Salvador, Monseñor Rosa Chávez, reported in February 1988 that members of the First Infantry Brigade were the perpetrators of a triple murder with all the characteristics of a "death squad" killing, he was immediately branded a criminal by the highest civilian and military authorities. It was up to the bishop to prove his "innocence." He was the accused, and it did not seem to matter much whether the facts he reported were really true or not.

4. Another element of falsehood is the degree of corruption that has increasingly permeated the various state organisms and the new Christian Democratic officials. Of course, this does not represent any historic novelty in a Salvadoran administration. What is new is that the corruption has penetrated so deeply into

a party that until recently had behaved with relative honesty and whose stated principles are strongly opposed to the private use of public resources. The overwhelming contrast between the political discourse and the actual behavior of the members of the Christian Democratic Party now in power establishes a new level of falsehood. This becomes all the more striking in the context of the Salvadoran people's present circumstances of extreme poverty. The most favorable judgment heard today about the corruption of the Christian Democrats in the government is that they are no different from governments previous to 1979—which were precisely those governments whose behavior helped bring about the civil war.

The Violence

It is known that the violence of war in El Salvador (as in the so-called low-intensity conflicts) has two sources: on the one hand, that of open military confrontation involving combatants; on the other, that of undercover paramilitary repression, directed not against combatants but against all sectors or groups of the population that support or sympathize with the insurgents or are suspected of supporting or sympathizing with them.

The Salvadoran war was previously characterized by a minimum of open military actions and a maximum of undercover paramilitary actions. The "death squads" rather than the battalions were the principal instruments of war used by the government to remain in power as it faced popular and revolutionary harassment. Nevertheless, with the prolongation of the war and the very demands of the United States' counterinsurgency project for El Salvador, this proportion has been inverted. While military confrontations have been acquiring primary importance, repression has been relegated to a minor position. Since 1984, there has been a significant reduction in the number of torture victims.

Nevertheless, two factual statements should be made:

1. The number of victims in military confrontations, including fatalities and the wounded, is currently much higher than the number of victims of repression.

2. The number of victims of repression has been reduced, but it is still higher than it was before the war, when it was con-

demned as unacceptable by international organizations such as the United Nations and the Organization of American States.

This change in the war's direction has given rise to a parallel phenomenon in the social order: an order maintained by state terrorism has given way to a militarized order. In El Salvador a militarization of society and of collective life has been produced, as much in the zones controlled by the government as in those controlled by the FMLN (although very clear differences exist between the two situations).

The militarization of the social order means, at the least, two things: (a) military officials tend to occupy most positions that are vital for institutional order; (b) military permission becomes the criterion of validity and even of possibility of any activity. In other words, it would be difficult to carry out any activity or business of any degree of importance in the country without obtaining the institutional endorsement of the armed forces or the personal sponsorship of some military officer. The surveillance the army openly exercises over the various systems of communication is nothing but the most visible expression of its growing power over the functioning of Salvadoran society.

PSYCHOSOCIAL TRAUMA

If human beings are products of history, then clearly the particular history of war in El Salvador will have repercussions on the mental health of its inhabitants. Here, this impact will be referred to as psychosocial trauma.

The Nature of Psychosocial Trauma Due to the War

Etymologically, trauma means injury. In psychology, it is customary to speak of trauma when referring to an experience that affects a person in such a way that he or she is scarred—that is, left with a permanent residue of what happened. If one speaks of trauma, it is because it is understood that this residue is negative, that an injury is involved that unfavorably marks the person's life.

In general, the term *psychic trauma* is used to refer to a particular injury that a difficult or exceptional experience—for example, the death of a beloved person, a situation of extreme stress or suffering, a painfully frustrating event—inflicts on a particular person. An example would be the experience of a child who sees his or her parents die in an accident or a fire. At times, in a sense more analogous to the Salvador situation, one speaks of *social trauma* to refer to the way in which some historic process can leave a whole population affected. This would be the case, for example, of the German people and of the Jewish people after the experience of the "final solution."

The term *psychosocial trauma* is not meant to express the idea that some uniform effect is produced throughout a population, or that one can assume in the experience of war some mechanical impact on people. The dialectical nature of psychosocial trauma implies that the injury or damage depends on the particular experience of each individual, an experience conditioned by his or her social background and degree of participation in the event and by other characteristics of the individual's personality and experience.[12] The suffering that accompanies war even offers some people the opportunity to grow in human terms. The development of someone like the martyred archbishop of San Salvador, Monseñor Oscar Arnulfo Romero, shows paradigmatically the growth of a person in proportion to the worsening of the persecution and attacks against him. Monseñor Romero is only one among many other Salvadorans to whom the war has given an opportunity to develop exceptional human virtues of pure altruism and love in solidarity with the Salvadoran people.

But in speaking of psychosocial trauma, one should emphasize two other aspects that are frequently forgotten: (a) the injury that affects people has been produced socially—i.e., its roots are not found in the individual, but in society; and (b) its very nature is nourished and maintained in the relationship between the individual and society, through various mediations by institutions, groups, and even individuals. These aspects have obvious important consequences that must be considered when trying to determine what ought to be done to overcome these traumas.

Psychosocial Trauma as Dehumanization

Joaquin Samayoa[13] holds that the cognitive and behavioral changes caused by war bring with them a process of dehumanization, understood as the impoverishment of four important abilities of the human being: (a) the ability to think lucidly, (b) the ability to communicate truthfully, (c) sensitivity to the suffering of others, and (d) hope.

What are the cognitive and behavioral changes caused by the necessity of adapting to war that bring about dehumanization? Samayoa mentions five: (1) selective inattention and a clinging to prejudices, (2) absolutism, idealization, and ideological rigidity, (3) evasive skepticism, (4) paranoid defensiveness, and (5) hatred and the desire for revenge. When examining how these cognitive and behavioral schemata emerge and how they are configured, Samayoa mentions three possible mechanisms: (a) insecurity about one's own fate, (b) the lack of purpose and even of meaning in what one does, and (c) the necessity of connection to or membership in some group.

A different line of thought has developed from the psychotherapeutic experience of the group in Chile headed by Elizabeth Lira.[14] This group suggests that a situation of state terrorism such as that undergone by Chile under Pinochet provokes a state of fear in people and, though fear is a subjective and, to a degree, a private experience, "upon being produced simultaneously in thousands of people in a society, it acquires an unsuspected relevance in social and political behavior."[15] According to this group of psychologists, there are four main psychological characteristics of the processes generated by this fear: (1) a sensation of vulnerability, (2) exacerbated alertness, (3) a sense of impotence or loss of control over one's own life, and (4) an altered sense of reality, making it impossible to objectively validate one's own experiences and knowledge.

The theories of Samayoa and of the Chilean group can be considered complementary: while one stresses the role of the cognitive and behavioral aspects, the other emphasizes the mediation of an affective element: fear. In this way, we have the three classic components of psychological analysis: knowledge, feelings, and behavior (for which some researchers substitute volition).

It is useful, nevertheless, to mention the limitations of both models. In the Chilean case, it is clear that the analysis is confined to those sectors of the population that have been the target of Pinochet's repression. Excluded would be persons favoring Pinochet, who rather than experiencing fear, have often gained satisfaction and increased security from a policy that guarantees their class dominance. Samayoa's focus is broader and, in principle, can be applied to all sectors of the population, since everyone has to adapt to historical circumstances. But it is precisely the fact of adaptation's being granted such a central role that is most unsatisfactory in this focus. It would seem that groups and individuals are external to the situation of war, to which they find themselves obliged to adapt. This would therefore involve a fundamentally reactive and even passive conception of how people face historical realities. The available evidence, however, leads to affirmation of the essentially active role groups and individuals play as subjects no matter how alienated they may be. There is no doubt that for many Salvadorans, the war is something imposed on them; but for a significant number, the war is something they themselves help to cause and develop. Looking at their participation in those processes from a merely adaptive perspective would lead to misunderstanding.

Crystallization of Social Relations

From my perspective, it appears that the best way to understand the psychosocial trauma currently experienced by the inhabitants of El Salvador is to conceive of it as the crystallization or materialization in individuals of the social relations of war that are experienced in the country. Obviously, underlying this proposition is an understanding of the human being as a product of a particular history, which in each case is manifested in the social relations of which the individual is an active and passive part.[16] From this we arrive at the notion that the nature of the primary social relations will be embodied in individuals. The role played by each of the psychic elements—knowledge, feelings, volition—should be examined individually; but in principle it is the whole of the individual that is affected by the experiences of these relationships of war. It follows that every person will be affected according to his or her particular social context and specific way of participating in the processes of war.

The psychosocial trauma that people experience entails the alienation of social relations. The human nature of the "enemies" is denied; one rejects the possibility of any constructive interaction with them, seeing them as something one would like to destroy. The affirmation of the personality itself is affected by the dehumanization of the other as it is dialectically constructed.

If the war in El Salvador is characterized by social polarization, the institutionalized lie, and the militarization of social life, then how these three predominant aspects of social relations are crystallized in individuals must be examined. This is not a question of looking for a mechanical correlation that would objectify what are nothing more than analytical aspects of a historical reality: it is a question of seeing how the specificity of the Salvadoran war marks groups and individuals—that is, how it is crystallized into a psychosocial trauma. What follow are some hypotheses that attempt to give an account of the disturbances that have been observed but that, as working hypotheses, should be subjected to empirical verification.

In the first place, it is hypothesized that the various forms of somaticization constitute the corporeal origins of social polarization. This is not to state that every polarizing process will necessarily take root in the organism, or that every psychosomatic disturbance should be attributed to the experience of the polarization of war. What is hypothesized is that the acute experience of polarization can, and frequently does, take root in the body itself.

It is not surprising, then, that the groups and individuals with the greatest propensity to experience this kind of disturbance are those who are most torn by the stresses of polarization: the inhabitants of places that continually go from being under the control of one side to control by the other, those who are subjected to an intense ideological bombardment by one side or the other without being able to state their own choice, and even those who have to force themselves to take extreme rigid positions in favor of the group to which they belong. Social disturbances correspond to personal and even somatic disturbances, and this can develop into the complex forms of psychotic alienation observed in some youths in the populations of conflictive areas.

In the second place, the prevailing climate of falsehood penetrates the bases of a person's identity in various ways. The clouding of reality generates a schizoid disjunction between subjective experience and social life that allows no room for the validating formalization of one's knowledge or, at best, refers it to an extremely restricted social circle. This difficulty in validating formalization of knowledge corresponds to a sense of insecurity about what one thinks and to skepticism regarding the various social and political options.

When falsehood must be adopted as a way of life and persons find themselves forced to lead a double existence—the case of those who work clandestinely—the problem is aggravated, not so much because there is no way to formalize and validate one's own experience as because the necessity of acting at two different levels can produce an ethical and experiential confusion. Many end up abandoning such a stressful life, which frequently produces a devaluation of the self-image and feelings of guilt regarding one's own convictions and one's old comrades. Lira and her colleagues have analyzed the problems of identity derived from the impossibility of organizing life according to one's own political values when those values are contrary to the established regime.[17]

Finally, the militarization of social life can create a progressive militarization of the mind. Again, this does not involve a simple or mechanical effect. But there is little doubt that the almost compulsive violence, which can dominate interpersonal relations, including the most intimate, and the sociopathic destructiveness manifested by some members or former members of the military forces are intrinsically related to the growing preponderance of military forms of thinking, feeling, and acting in social life. The most serious effect of this psychosocial militarization occurs when it becomes a normal way of being that is transmitted by the processes of socialization, as in the case of the children who ingenuously affirm that the way to get rid of poverty is by killing all the poor.

CONCLUSION: THE PSYCHOSOCIAL TASK AT HAND

The indefinite prolongation of the war in El Salvador presumes the normalization of these kinds of dehumanized social relationships, whose impact ranges from somatic stress to the rending of mental structures and the weakening of the personality, which can find no way of authentically affirming its own identity. It is thus impossible to understand organic crises without reference to polarizing tension. Similarly, sociopolitical inhibition cannot be understood except in response to the institutionalized lie, or the stereotypical ideologue except in response to the militarization of social life. But persons who are formed in this context assume an inherent contempt for human life, adhere to the law of the strongest (or the most violent) as a social criterion, and accept corruption as a lifestyle, thus precipitating a vicious circle that tends to perpetuate the war — objectively as well as subjectively.

I have made no attempt to discuss here ways of dealing with this problem. But any reckoning shows the inadequacy of psychotherapy, whether individual or group, understood as a process of psychological intervention. This does not mean that the people who suffer the alienating havoc of Salvadoran history should be abandoned to their fate. The point is that psychotherapy is insufficient, even in the case of the very people who are involved. So long as there is no significant change in social relations (structural, group, and interpersonal) as they exist today in El Salvador, individual treatment of their consequences would be at best incomplete.

In El Salvador it is necessary to begin an intensive effort to depolarize, demilitarize, and de-ideologize the country, in order to heal social relations and allow people to work out their history in a better kind of interpersonal context. Stated in positive terms, it is necessary to work toward establishing a new framework for coexistence, a new "social contract" that would allow collective interaction without turning disagreement into mutual negation. There is an urgent need to work toward a process of greater social sincerity, in order to learn about realities before defining them, to accept facts before interpreting them. Finally, an effort must be made to educate by reason, not by force, so that coexistence can be based on mutually complementary efforts employed to resolve problems, not on violence used to impose one's own alternative.

NOTES

1. Instituto de Derechos Humanos (IDHUCA), *Los derechos humanos en El Salvador en 1986* (San Salvador: Universidad Centroamericana José Simeón Cañas, 1987); idem, *Los derechos humanos en El Salvador en 1987* (1988); idem, *Los Derechos económicos, sociales y culturales en El Salvador* (1988); J. F. Kerry, *El Salvador Update: Counterterrorism in Action* (Los Angeles: El Rescate Human Rights Department, 1987).

2. Asociación de Capacitación e Investigación para la Salud Mental (ACISAM), "Presencia del Ejército en el refugio de San José Calle Real: Una vivencia amedrentadora," *Avance* (San Salvador), January 1988, p. 8.

3. R. L. Leahy, ed., *The Child's Construction of Social Inequality* (New York: Academic Press, 1983).

4. T. P. Anderson, *Matanza: El Salvador's Communist Revolt of 1932* (Lincoln: University of Nebraska Press, 1971).

5. IDHUCA, *Los derechos económicos, sociales y culturales en El Salvador* (1988).

6. I. Martín-Baró, "El Salvador 1987," *Estudios Centroamericanos* (ECA), no. 471–72 (1988), pp. 21–45.

7. I. Martín-Baró, "Guerra y salud mental," *Estudios Centroamericanos,* no. 429–30 (1984), pp. 503–14.

8. A. J. Bacevich, J. D. Hallums, R. H. White, and T. F. Young, *American Military Policy in Small Wars: The Case of El Salvador* (John F. Kennedy School of Government, March 22, 1988).

9. American Psychiatric Association, *Diagnostic and Statistical Manual of Mental Disorders,* 3rd ed. (Washington, D.C.: American Psychiatric Association, 1980).

10. Martín-Baró, "Guerra y salud mental," p. 507.

11. *Debate Nacional 1988 convocado por el Arzobispado de San Salvador, del 17 de junio al 4 de septiembre de 1988* (San Salvador: Arzobispado).

12. Martín-Baró, "Guerra y salud mental," pp. 509–11.

13. J. Samayoa, "Guerra y deshumanización: Una perspectiva psicosocial," *Estudios Centroamericanos,* n. 461 (1987), pp. 213–25.

14. E. Lira, "Consecuencias psicosociales de la represión en Chile," *Revista de Psicologia de El Salvador,* n. 28 (1988), p. 143; E. Lira, E. Weinstein, R. Dominquez, J. Kovalskys, A. Maggi, E. Morales, and F. Pollarolo, *Psicoterapia y represión política* (Mexico City: Siglo XXI, 1984); E. Lira, E. Weinstein, and S. Salamovich, "El miedo: Un

enfoque psicosocial," *Revista chilena de psicologia,* 8 (1985–86), p. 51; Fundación de Ayuda Social de las Iglesias Cristianas (FASIC), *Exilio 1986–1988* (Santiago: Amerinda, 1988); E. Weinstein, E. Lira et al., *Trauma, duelo y reparación. Una experiencia de trabajo psicosocial en Chile* (Santiago: FASIC/Interamericana, 1987).

15. Lira, Weinstein, Salamovich, "El miedo," p. 51.

16. I. Martín-Baró, *Acción e ideologia. Psicologia social desde Centroamérica* (San Salvador: UCA Editores, 1983).

17. Lira, "Consequencias psicosociales"; Lira, Weinstein, Dominquez et al., *Psicoterapia;* Lira, Weinstein, Salamovich, "El miedo"; FASIC, *Exilio;* Weinstein, Lira, Rojas et al., *Trauma;* E. Weinstein, "Prolemática psicológica del exilio en Chile. Algunas orientaciones psicoterapéuticas," *Boletín de Psicologia* (San Salvador), 23 (1987), p. 21.

∽ 4 ∽

Juan Ramón Moreno, S.J.

"Pardito"
b. Aug. 29, 1933; d. Nov. 16, 1989
Assistant Director, Oscar Romero Center

As a novice, "Pardito" boasted of being worldly, and when the others would kid him, he laughed at them for having come from minor seminaries or other hothouses. Ironically, life took him down pathways of spirituality, and his principal "public" came to be priests and sisters, as well as fellow Jesuits.

He had not done special studies, as had most of those martyred with him, so he didn't have a doctorate or even a master's.

Pardito was nonetheless able and intelligent, both precise and profound, if not so creative. At any rate, his lack of a doctorate had nothing to do with ability. He never got a chance to do higher studies.

He started out in biology. That was his forte. For three years as a young Jesuit, he taught it in the high school of the San Salvador seminary. At the same time, however, he had to jump from subject to subject, no matter how disparate from one another: history, civics, math, English, geography. As the years went by, he gave up biology, but he kept an interest in science as it touched on philosophy, and in bioethics especially. He had a taste for exactitude. (Who would have thought so, looking at his messy desk?) He had become an expert in computers by the time he was killed, and he had already modernized the library catalog system at the Center of Theological Reflection.

He got a good grounding in the principles of Ignatian spirituality from his novice master, Miguel Elizondo, who left his spiritual mark on five of the six slain Jesuits. But Pardito did not have to concentrate on studying these principles till he himself was named novice master—at precisely the moment (1969) of the great changes in the order in Central America. Those were to be his tough years, for the new formation was just starting to jell, and nearly all his novices later left the order. That weighed on him a lot.

From this period dates his commitment to the intramural life of the Society of Jesus: He was a Province consultor, gave classes in the novitiate and juniorate, served as secretary to the Provincial and edited the Province newsletter. And he made Ignatian spirituality his specialty. While in Panama, he founded an Ignatian Center, and he took it with him when he was transferred to Managua, Nicaragua. He started the magazine *Diakonia,* which was indeed, as the name denotes, a "service" for religious. In it he gathered others' articles. He hardly ever wrote himself. The pen was not his charism, or perhaps it was, but he seemed to feel overshadowed by others.

His charism was preaching. Although somewhat self-effacing, he caught fire when he spoke in public and became strongly persuasive. He gave many, many retreats to priests and religious, including Jesuits. His approach was quite dynamic, really—along the lines of liberation theology—but even though these ideas were incendiary, his manner was reassuring because he knew how to ground social commitment in spirituality and faith. People had confidence in him because he was not "radical." No wonder then that, wherever he went, he became influential among the conferences of religious, and he was elected president of these conferences in both Panama and Nicaragua.

Unlike others of his companion martyrs, he had not put down deep roots in any one country of Central America, since those roots were really to be found in the world of religious. Nor was he one who had a lot of lay friends to visit. This was due partly to shyness, partly to his having moved from country to country. Perhaps his closest such friendships were among the people near Boaco, Nicaragua, where he had lived for several intense months during the literacy crusade of 1980.

At the Central American University in San Salvador, he served as librarian for the Center of Theological Reflection and assistant director of the Oscar Romero Center, whose offices and library were on the first floor of the building where the murder took place. As part of the slaughter, the soldiers firebombed the filing cabinets, destroyed the computers and also, apparently, wiped out all the information Pardito had stored on disks and tapes.

Evangelization in the Contemporary World

"Evangelization" is a complex term. On the basis of the word itself, we could define it as the communication of good news. But it is the convergence of a number of diverse things that make good news both news and good: its source, content, bearer, recipient, what it is about this news that makes it good for this recipient, and so forth.

Moreover, what I want to clarify here is to some degree not evangelization in general, but *Christian* evangelization. Not just any "good news" proclaimed is Christian, nor is just any way of proclaiming it Christian.

Importance of the Issue

This issue is crucially important. That is why it is so insistently raised in living communities within the church, whether directly or in the form of questions on the mission of the church, religious life, base communities, or the parish. The official magisterium of the church has also devoted special attention to this issue: the 1974 synod, *Evangelii Nuntiandi*, the Puebla conference, the focus of the celebration of the five hundredth anniversary of the European discovery of Latin America, in which the emphasis falls on "new evangelization," are but expressions of a deep concern.

It could not be otherwise, if, as was stated at the 1974 synod and repeated in *Evangelii Nuntiandi*, "the task of the evangelization of all human beings constitutes the essential mission of the church," and if, as Paul VI insists, "to evangelize is the joy and particular calling of the church, its deepest identity. It exists in order to evangelize" (EN, 14). Thus it is clear that in evangelization the church's very raison d'être is at stake and, accordingly, that of religious life and of all movements of Christian

This essay originally appeared in the *Revista Latinoamericana de Teología* (September-December, 1988), which is published by the Jesuits in San Salvador. The translation is by Phillip Berryman.

life. Consequently, evangelization is not one issue among the various issues that can and must be considered, but is itself the central issue. When we inquire about what it means to evangelize, we are inquiring about the very essence of the church.

I think this is now quite clear in the awareness of the church and in our own awareness as men and women seeking to live out our Christian and ecclesial vocation in religious life. Perhaps however, we should clarify more what this demands of the church and of the various ecclesial institutions.

Difficulties and Demands

Today we encounter particular diffculties in evangelizing the modern world, but if we intend to be honest we have to ask ourselves: Are these difficulties simply the product of the resistance and particular obstacles raised by the world today, such as atheism, secularism, consumerism, hedonism, and all the other "isms" that could be added on? Or might they also be the product of a church that has not proved itself capable of shaping itself and structuring its pastoral work in a way that might invigorate its ability to transmit credibly to today's men and women the good news of Jesus?

No one denies that a changed world requires new ways of evangelizing, but does it not also demand a new way of being church, and for us within the church, a new style of religious life? How are we to be good news for today's world? The church is not something that is first built in itself and then receives the gospel to transmit after it is already set up. Not at all. In its very constitution the church is mission and its mission is to evangelize. The church of Jesus is set apart and established in the very act of evangelizing. The Holy Spirit, bringing the church to birth, is given as a power for carrying out this mission. "As the Father has sent me, so I send you" (John 20:21). "You will receive power when the Holy Spirit comes down on you; then you are to be my witnesses in Jerusalem, throughout Judea and Samaria, yes, even to the ends of the earth" (Acts 1:8).

The aim is to give witness to Jesus, God's definitive gospel. The oldest gospel we know bears this title: "Beginning of the good news of Jesus, the Christ" (Mark 1:1). But we should not forget that before being the Christ who is proclaimed, he is the

Jesus who proclaims, the Jesus who evangelizes. One of the merits of *Evangelii Nuntiandi* is that it sheds light on the topic of evangelization through Jesus, "the first and greatest evangelizer" (EN, 6). This leads to an understanding of evangelization not in the abstract, but out of the historic embodiment that is Jesus of Nazareth. It is by looking at Jesus that the church learns to be evangelizing.

JESUS AND EVANGELIZATION

The Principle and Foundation of Evangelization

The first thing we must learn is what comes *first* in evangelization. First not simply in the chronological sense, but in a radical sense: what is most at the source, the root from which the whole evangelization process springs and at the same time sustains and nourishes it; its principle and foundation—that is, that which grounds and gives origin to evangelization by being the principle of a way of being and acting, which, precisely because it has such a foundation, becomes good news.

When Jesus, answering the scribe who asks which commandment is most basic, offers the parable of the Samaritan, he gives us important clues for understanding what it means to evangelize, to become good news. For that man, attacked by bandits on the way to Jericho and left half-dead, the priest who saw him, and took a wide detour around him and kept going, was not good news, nor was the Levite who passed by later. The one who was good news was the Samaritan, who was able to understand his situation of need, be moved by it, and take effective action to save the man and provide for his needs.

I am going to take the liberty of pausing over this parable to analyze what is essential about it. Lying on the roadway is this wounded man on the verge of losing his life. Suddenly the Samaritan comes on the scene and the Gospel text says he was "moved with pity at the sight. He approached him and dressed his wounds, pouring on oil and wine. He then hoisted him on his own beast and brought him to an inn, where he cared for him." It all begins with his being moved with pity "at the sight," the act of looking, becoming aware of a presence there. But that becoming aware of a suffering and needy presence does not in itself lead to hope and joy; it is not automatically good news. The priest and the Levite passing by also "saw," but their way of looking, and what fell within their glance, could not inspire the subsequent steps leading to good news: they "saw him, but continued on." Looking is not enough; what is behind the gaze is crucial, and consequently the Samaritan and the two servants of the temple have diffent ways of looking, different eyes. The latter two look without solidarity, from a distance, and do not let themselves be affected by the situation of the other, who simply does not arouse enough interest in them to make them go through the trouble of changing their travel plans and coming forward. They do not have compassionate love, the ability to become concerned over the situation of other persons, and in view of their precarious situation, to become involved. The Samaritan's gaze is very different — the gaze of one who is open to the situation of others, because he has a heart of solidarity, because he is capable of committed love. Consequently what his gaze captures in suffering, in excruciating reality, affects him to the point where he is "moved to pity."

Luke here uses the Greek verb *splanchnizomai*, which the Gospels repeatedly apply to Jesus. Literally it means that one's guts are stirred. And one's guts are affected when there is some- thing foreign irritating them, something that must be expelled and gotten rid of, if one is to be at rest. This is *compassion* in the strong sense of the word. Solidarity with others leads to being identified with them so that their pain, their passion, become one's own (com-passion), and they pain one to the point of being unbearable: they have to be relieved, something must be done to change the situation of suffering. That leads to action, to doing something that relieves the suffering of the other, which is also one's own suffering.

Consequently, the parable here tells us that the Samaritan "approached him." Being identified with the other in solidarity leads him to move and come foward, to make himself neighbor to the other, to enter into his world in order to be able to familiarize himself with his need and deal with it. But this demands leaving one's own world, one's own interests and con- cerns, to change one's own plans, in order to adjust to what serving the other's life demands. The Samaritan puts aside his travel plans in order to enter into the situation of suffering of the wounded man, to become involved with him and take him toward curing, toward life. He has proved capable of becoming good news for the man assaulted by robbers. The only grammar in which the Christian good news can be expressed is the grammar of merciful love, the grammar of solidarity with the other. And at the root, at the originating source of this good news, are the innermost recesses of mercy.

It is significant that this way of acting, which Jesus presents as a model ("go and do the same"), simply reflects Jesus' own way of acting. It is striking how often the gospel describes for us Jesus' activity through a set of three gestures inseparably interconnected: "Jesus looked at him with love and told him . . ." (Mark 10:21), "he saw the vast throng, his heart was moved with pity, and he cured their sick" (Matt 14:14). Before speaking or acting comes the gesture of looking, expressing a heart of mercy, a concern to penetrate reality, as crude as it is, without evading anything. When this situation of the other person is a situation of suffering, the heart allows itself to be affected by this suffering and looking becomes compassion.

This gaze falls most frequently on what the gospels call *ochlos*, crowd, mass. In Matthew chapter 4, at the outset of Jesus' public life, when the evangelist presents one of those summaries, which are subsequently repeated and pull together what is most basic in Jesus' messianic activity, we read:

> His reputation traveled the length of Syria. They carried to him all those afflicted with various diseases and racked with pain: the possessed, the lunatics, the paralyzed. He cured them all. The great crowds that followed him came from Galilee, the ten cities, Jerusalem and Judea, and from across the Jordan [4:24–25].

Mark chapter 3 further describes this multitude as pressing in on Jesus so much so that he asks them to ready a boat lest he be overwhelmed. "Because he had cured many, all who had afflictions kept pushing toward him to touch him" (3:10). This is no doubt a suffering multitude, a multitude of the ragged, the needy and the sick, who discover in Jesus something that awakens hope within them: there is something in Jesus that tells them that their situation of suffering can be changed, that things are going to change. In their anguish they seek out Jesus to the point where they are pressing in on him and not even leaving him room to eat, as the evangelist notes later on. In fact when Jesus at one point, seeking a moment of relief, asks them to take him across the lake in a boat, the crowd is already there waiting for him. "When he disembarked and saw the vast throng, his heart was moved with pity, and he cured their sick" (Matt 14:14).

This is the world to which Jesus draws near, the one he enters, and over whose situation he allows himself to be moved, and which he commits himself to change. When John's disciples ask him if he is the one who is to come, his answer is, "Look and give witness to what you have seen and heard." What have they seen and heard? That things are changing, "the lame walk, the blind see, the dead rise, and the poor hear the good news" (Cf. Matt 11:3–6). There is a change in the situation that engenders life and hence engenders hope. It is compassion seeking to effectively change what is preventing the other person from living.

The "Good News" of the Incarnation

In trying to understand what the good news means from the perspective of the overall mystery of the incarnation, we encounter the same root from which springs the possibility of the good news: mercy. When St. Ignatius Loyola in his *Spiritual Exercises* presents contemplation on the incarnation, a key passage for understanding Ignatian and Jesuit spirituality, he sets up as it were an opposition between the world affected by sin and the trinitarian God looking at this world. It is a world without solidarity, a lost world, a world without hope. And God looks at this world in the only way God knows how to look: with the Father's gaze, with a look that arises out of loving concern over what happens in the world. And despite what this gaze sees, and just because of what it sees, there wells up in God's heart — so to speak — compassionate tenderness; God's merciful heart is stirred. "God so loved the world that he gave his only Son" (John 3:16). St. Paul will say: "It is precisely in this that God proves his love for us: that while we were still sinners, Christ died for us" (Rom 8:5). God's response to this world stretched out on the roadside, this world in the throes of a despairing death, is, as in the parable of the Samaritan, to come close to the world, to enter into the world: "the Word became flesh and made his dwelling among us" (John 1:14). Love is what brings together whatever can be brought together in our history of nonsolidarity, suffering, and frustration, but not in order to leave that history as it is, but to transform it, to make it be what it should be. It will no longer be possible to find God outside human history, and outside the struggle to make that history shot through with God, a history of salvation.

Thus the good news exists simply because God is a God with a heart of mercy, a God who seeks our good not because we are God but because God is good, who loves us not because we are lovable but because God is love. And this mercy acts by coming close, by taking on solidarity, by being identified with the one who is loved and who thus receives the good news that something basic is going to change in his or her situation.

St. Paul uses the expression of self-emptying to describe this movement. It means entering into the other's little world, taking on the limitation of human flesh. The uncreated word, which was together with God, which was God, now becomes human word, expresses itself in Aramaic, becomes incarnate in a specific culture, enters into one people's history. This movement also supposes a moment of passivity: to become flesh is to allow oneself to be given flesh. In every drawing near, there is a moment of receiving, of allowing oneself to be taught by the other who offers me his or her reality. In Mary's virginal womb, the Word accepts being given a body, a historic and human body. And this human flesh will be born small and limited, as is true of all human flesh. The newborn child, who, wrapped in swaddling clothes as a symbol of his weakness, has to be raised and taught, has to be aided to "grow in wisdom, grace, and age," expresses with amazing adaptability what it means to become incarnate.

Both Matthew and Luke, the two evangelists of infancy narratives, attach a great deal of importance to the genealogy of Jesus, although in different perspectives. The genealogies, which may be tedious and rather meaningless for a modern reader, are for the evangelists the way to express that the incarnation demands being inserted into the life of a lineage, a specific people, in this case the Jewish people, from which one receives one's history and culture, and whose fate one takes on. To take on a real body is to become incorporated into the struggles and hopes of a people on the march. The author of the Letter to the Hebrews powerfully describes this movement in solidarity with the incarnation by stating that Jesus "was tempted in every way that we are, yet never sinned" (Heb 4:15).

The importance of this moment of passivity for Jesus — allowing himself to be given a body, a culture, a human identity — comes out sharply in the more than thirty years of silence and obscurity he spends in Nazareth. All Jesus' activity is simply that of one more person within his people. Only after he has allowed himself to be given speech, when he has been thoroughly imbued with his people's way of being, does he go out, moved by the Spirit, to openly carry out his messianic activity. Indeed his first public act will be that of standing in solidarity with the sinful people, and as one more among them, receiving the baptism of penance from John's hands.

Being "Good News" in a Divided World: Partiality toward the Poor

Going on now to focus on Jesus' public activity, it seems quite clear that the fundamental horizon within which that whole activity unfolds is what Jesus calls the reign of God. As the synoptic Gospels indicate, what Jesus proclaims is the reign of God as a something approaching, which, when it breaks into history, will change it at the root. It is especially important that the center of Jesus' preaching is not simply God but God's reign. The God of Jesus is not disinterested in what goes on in the world, but on the contrary is concerned over what takes place in history and is affected by the situation of humankind even to the point of becoming part of that history through the incarnation, as we have just noted.

But this is a divided world, and in a divided world the good news must inevitably be partial. It does not ring the same in everybody's ears. Already in the Jewish context in which Jesus carries out his mission, the proclamation of the approaching reign evokes the presence of a God who comes to do justice, to make things be as they should be. In every society there are strong and weak, powerful and impotent. As a result of the nonsolidarity of the human heart, most often the powerful use force to take advantage of the weak, violating their dignity and crushing their rights. The weak have no way to defend their rights; they can only die or be resigned to bearing the oppression and abuse imposed on them by the selfishness of the powerful. This unleashes a logic within history in which the powerful become ever more powerful by making the weak ever weaker and ever more subject to the whim of the strong. The idea of a just king who comes to effectively exercise his sovereignty entails his coming to establish justice by defending the rights of the poor and weak, who have no way of making that right effective.

That is precisely what the Hebrew expression *malkuth Yahweh*, reign of Yahweh, evokes in the minds of the Israelites listening to Jesus. When they were liberated from slavery in Egypt, the people of God experienced God's justice-bearing action. But when oppressive abuses, and the scandalous division into poor and rich, appear amid the people of Israel, Yahweh again comes to the defense of the weak—orphans, widows, emigrants, day laborers, the poor—to make their right respected. So much is God seen to be taking sides with the poor—not only in the prophetic books—that there are even texts in the Old Testament that describe Yahweh to us not so much as a judge pronouncing sentence, but as one of the parties in court, taking on the defense of the poor and the oppressed, and accusing the rich oppressor. A quick reading of Psalm 72, a psalm of royal enthronement, is enough to grasp its understanding of a just king:

> He shall defend the afflicted among the
>   people,
> save the children of the poor,
> and crush the oppressor . . . .
> For he shall rescue the poor man when
>   he cries out,
> and the afflicted when he has no one to
>   help him.

> He shall have pity for the lowly and the
>   poor;
> the lives of the poor he shall save.

Hence, when Jesus proclaims that the reign of God is coming, what he is announcing is the exercise of God's sovereign mercy, which in an unjust world takes the form of implanting justice, and effectively recognizing the rights of the impoverished. This will entail a radical change in the situation of the poor, who until now have been condemned to inhuman living conditions, to die before their time and see their loved ones die before their time, clearly as a result of the arrogance and exploitation of the powerful. Naturally the change cannot but resound as good news, as great news, in the ears of the poor. Here is the meaning of the saying "Blessed are you who are poor, for yours is the reign of God." It means the proclamation of the end of their unjust oppression, the source of so much suffering and death. Things are going to change, for the better.

That the situation of the poor really changes, that the tears of those who weep will be dried, that the poor will leap for joy over the good news Jesus brings, thus constitute Jesus' progra-matic presentation of his mission and the fundamental criterion for recognizing him as messiah:

> The spirit of the Lord is upon me:
> therefore he has anointed me.
> He has sent me to bring glad tidings to
>   the poor [Luke 4:18].

> Go back and report to John what you hear
>   and see [Matt 11:4].

If what is proclaimed is not good news for the poor, it is not the gospel of Jesus. Hence the initial response the proclamation of the reign produces within the poor is one of joy and happiness. Later there will be a call to live up to the values of the coming reign, by allowing God's merciful love to fill and transform them, but first they must feel the consolation of this presence that ends the causes of their affliction. The first word that the oppressed adulterous woman hears from Jesus is "No one has condemned you; you may go." But to receive God's mercy is a call to become merciful; the next line is "from now on, sin no more" (John 8:11).

The Dilemma of the Rich

But this change in the situation of the poor has to take place in a context where there is a causal, dialectical relationship between poverty and wealth. Basically the poor are *impoverished* due to hoarding and exploitation by the rich; and the rich are *enriched* at the cost of the impoverishment and misery of the masses. To free the poor by giving them access to living conditions consonant with their dignity as human beings and children of God entails sacrificing the privileges of wealthy oppressors. Hence when faced with the news that the reign of God is coming, the rich feel challenged and called to accept God's justice and kindness, by allowing themselves to be re-created and changed by that justice into brothers and sisters, and persons in solidarity. "Be converted and believe the good news" (Mark 1:15). Only conversion, *metanoia*, change of mentality, new eyes in order to see reality with love in solidarity with which God views it, can enable the approach of the reign to ring out as good news in the ears of the rich—conversion to the God who comes in gratuity and kindness to remake things, to the God of the reign.

But to be converted to this God is to be converted to the poor and their cause: "What you do to one of these, you do to me." And this conversion is hard, it is a frightfully radical change that demands that one be decentered, abandon the viewpoint of one's own interests and privileges, whether individual or of class or nation, in order to take a stand in favor of the interests of the poor. "I give half my belongings, Lord, to the poor. If I have defrauded anyone in the least, I pay him back fourfold" (Luke 19:8). At that point the reign of God becomes good news for Zacchaeus and salvation enters his house.

But what happens when the privileged, who monopolize wealth, knowledge, and power, take advantage of their strength to stubbornly defend their privileges and refuse to be converted to this God who is in solidarity with the poor? Jesus bluntly describes the inescapable choice: "You cannot serve God and money." After hearing Jesus' loving request, to "Go, sell what you have, and give to the poor," the rich young man's "face fell. He went away sad, for he had many possessions" (Mark 10:21–22). For him Jesus' word becomes bad news that makes him sad.

But even worse, the approach of the reign that is coming to change the state of things in favor of the poor is seen as a threat to the interests of the rich. It interferes with the law of dog-eat-dog, with the law of selfishness. And the rich, clinging to their privileges, are not going to allow that: these dangerous edges of the gospel will have to be blunted and it will have to be reduced to spiritualistic discourse that has no impact on reality, or it will have to be silenced permanently. Jesus' life is marked by conflict with the socio-religious and religious powers of his age, because he stubbornly insists on not announcing a God without the reign, but a God committed to the life of the poor. Religious challenge likewise becomes social challenge, and hence subversion, seeking to restructure society as God wants it. The powers of the world undertake a war to the death against this way of conceiving God, against this good news to the poor. Jesus ends up being crucified.

How is it possible that God's goodness, acting humanly in Jesus, should provoke this rejection and aggression to the point of death, and death on a cross? The parable of the good shepherd sheds light on this question. A good shepherd is one who is concerned for the life of the sheep, and precisely out of that concern, is devoted to providing effective protection for their weakness. But what makes the good shepherd *good* is that he "gives his life for his sheep." Being concerned for the life of the sheep and giving one's life for them are inseparable; they are the essential traits of the good shepherd. Why? Because there are wolves who feed off the death of the sheep. When the good shepherd steps in to defend the sheep, the destructive power of the wolf falls on him, not because the wolf is concerned with the shepherd himself but rather because the shepherd prevents him from getting at his prey. If the good shepherd could be bought off or intimidated, there would be no need to do away with him. But the good shepherd is the one who, as Archbishop Romero said—and he made it real with his own blood—"does not want security as long as it does not provide security for his flock."

WORD AND DEED: THE CONTEXT OF EVANGELIZATION

Having considered at least briefly the fundamental content of evangelization and how this content affects its bearer and its addressees, let me now say a word about how evangelization should be carried out in the concrete.

I have repeatedly emphasized that what comes first is mercy, the love that lets itself be affected by the other's situation. After Jesus sees and lets himself be moved by what he sees, his impulse of solidarity seeks to remedy the pressing situation of the other, and to communicate life to those who are prevented from living. But how to carry out this task?

The synoptics summarize Jesus' evangelizing activity with this basic description: "he went about . . . proclaiming the good news of the reign, curing every kind of illness and disease." Proclaiming the good news in words has been the usual, and until recently practically the only way of understanding evangelization. No doubt transmitting the gospel message through preaching, catechesis, liturgical celebration, and so forth is an essential element in the task of evangelization. It is the word that illuminates the meaning of events; it is the word that makes the good news heard and issues the invitation to accept it through conversion; it is the word that explicitates and celebrates the hidden presence of God in the course of history: it is the word that unmasks and denounces the antireign powers of resisting its transforming power.

But in order to be evangelizing, to be good news, the word must be effective; a word that in some manner effects what it announces, an existential word that, like the uncreated Word, becomes incarnate in history and transforms it from within. In Jesus the word is accompanied by concrete deeds that make it real by transforming reality and effectively communicating life: "the lame walk, the blind see, the dead rise." It is these deeds that give the word its credibility, as anticipations *already* communicating life, although they are not the fullness of life: deeds that liberate from oppression, although they are not the final and complete liberation from all slavery; deeds that are an active presence of the reign, although they are not the eschatological and definitive incursion of the reign.

But word and deeds are the existential dimensions through which the primary reality of all evangelization, compassionate and merciful love, becomes embodied in history. It is this love that sometimes becomes word and at other times becomes deed, or both at once, in accordance with the concrete situation of those to whom it is addressed. Again it is enlightening to see how often the evangelists connect the gesture of *seeing* with all Jesus' activity, including preaching or issuing a personal challenge: "seeing the crowd . . . he taught them saying . . ."; "Looking at him, he loved him and he said to him . . ." Evangelizing is not repeating or having others memorize set formulas, as polished as they might seem. Evangelizing is saying the word needed, the word that is indeed good news in the existential situation in which addressees find themselves. Evangelizing means changing the situation so that others can live the life that is theirs as human persons and children of God.

Whether the accent is to fall more on word or deeds will depend on the situation in which we are trying to make God's goodness present. When the Samaritan is lying unconscious on the road, what is useful right away is not a word, but action to save his life and heal his wounds. The moment will come, however, when the words can be heard and can help shed light on the deep meaning of some events in which God's loving mercy acting salvifically through the one who was capable of becoming a brother or sister has become present, even though no attention has hitherto been paid to that presence.

Word and deeds are both the concrete expression in history of what Jesus is: the clear visibility in human flesh of God's mercy; a concerned love that comes to liberate and communicate life. Of Jesus it is said that he "went about" places; his love does not remain still but is an impatient love from which there flows a way of being and acting that is in itself good news. That Jesus is this way, that he speaks as he speaks, that he accepts the poor and sinners as he accepts them, that he stands up to the powers that be as he does, that he strives and wearies himself going about the roads of Palestine, that he forgives as he forgives the sinful woman and those who crucify him, that he dies as he does and rises as he does—in a word, that Jesus is as he is, is good news. In his humanity, in what he is, there appears the very being, the very goodness and tenderness, of God: "Whoever sees me, sees the Father" (John 14:9). The God seen in Jesus is not the arbitrary God who imposes fear and punishes those who violate the established order, but the God who is close at hand and accepting, who more than anything else wants human beings to live, and especially those whom the sinful structures of the world do not let live: the poor and the humble. The whole Jesus event is good news.

Although I believe that what I have been saying up to this point sheds considerable light on the path we should follow as evangelizers today, I am going to try to spell out some aspects that may be more relevant in our present context.

Characteristics of Today's World

Without the slightest intention of being exhaustive, I am going to go over in summary fashion some of the characteristic traits of this contemporary world of ours in which we must carry out our vocation to evangelize.

To begin with, there is the phenomenon of the globalization of history. The enormous advance of communications has so shortened distances that for the first time we can speak correctly of *one* humankind, *one* history, and of social, economic, and political problems that are *common* to all humankind. A decision is made in the Kremlin or in the White House, and there is a great deal of suffering in Afghanistan, Central America, Angola, or the Middle East. President Reagan sneezes in Washington and the great stock exchanges in Europe, Asia, or the Americas tremble. The International Monetary Fund stubbornly maintains an economic policy, and hundreds of miners and workers in Bolivia, Brazil, or Argentina are thrown into unemployment and hunger. The spread of international organizations, headed by the United Nations, clearly expresses the extent and importance of this phenomenon.

Paralleling such phenomena we find the rapid advance of science and technology, which is leading to the spectacular domination over nature that humankind is acquiring. The resulting spread of technology is unquestionably improving the quality of life of many men and women, and is arousing new hope in others. However, this is a technology monopolized and jealously guarded — at least in its most advanced levels — by the most powerful societies. The consequence is an increasing distance separating the strong from the weak, and the appearance of new instruments and forms of oppression and exploitation.

Ours is an overdeveloped world with an impressive supply of consumer goods and services, but one in which there are more poor than ever. In his recent social encyclical John Paul II states:

> Without going into an analysis of figures and statistics, it is sufficient to face squarely the reality of an *innumerable multitude of people* — children, adults and the elderly — in other words, real and unique human persons, who are suffering under the intolerable burden of poverty. There are many millions who are deprived of hope due to the fact that, in many parts of the world, their situation has noticeably worsened [*Sollictudo Rei Socialis*, 13].

Despite providing the technical possibility to do so, this development without solidarity has not been able to eradicate the dire poverty that condemns so many millions of human beings to early deaths.

Our world is marked by the lack of solidarity and the mistrust of people toward each other. A world is divided into blocs or groups whose interests are in conflict: east-west, north-south, capital-labor, rich-poor, Jews-Arabs, oppressive races-oppressed races. . . . They are different worlds within the one world. Today we speak of a First World, a Second World, a Third World, and even a Fourth World — worlds with quite opposite situations and conditions. A study made in 1983 sponsored by the Rockefeller Foundation and other respected institutions estimated that since the last world war there have been some 125 major armed conflicts, 95 of them in the Third World, resulting in many millions of deaths. Just in Central America more than two hundred thousand persons have been murdered since 1978, many of them horribly mutilated. The 1985 arms production reached $663 billion, almost $2 billion a day, which is itself triple the average annual budget of a country like El Salvador, while in the world every day fifty thousand children die of sheer malnutrition.

It is true that dozens of nations previously subject to the whim of empires have moved into political independence in recent years, but it is also true that instead of becoming autonomous and intent on moving toward participating justly in the goods and services destined for all, they become cogs in a huge machine. A new form of imperialism has arisen.

A plague typifying and revealing the imbalances and conflicts of the contemporary world are the millions of refugees whose "tragedy . . . is reflected in the hopeless faces of men, women, and children who can no longer find a home in a divided and inhospitable world" (*Sollicitudo Rei Socialis*, 24). To these are to be added the illegal immigrants subject to the greatest dangers and humiliations, rejected by a society that is afraid of seeing its own living standards lowered if it has to share its goods and resources with others.

I could certainly go on listing further characteristics: terrorism, foreign debt, illiteracy, discrimination, unemployment, drugs. All of them contribute to reinforcing the image of a world that as a whole is inhospitable and inhumane, a devastating world that has nothing in common with the project of a Father who wants us all to be brothers and sisters. It is a world where, if in personal matters there can be and is human sensitivity and solidarity, on structural levels, both national and international, the law of the jungle still prevails. "Our vital interests," "the security of the nation," and so forth, are the high-sounding words that conceal the idols of death. The real enemy of the God of Jesus is not the atheism that denies God's existence, but far more this idolatry that sacrifices millions of human victims before the altar of power and money.

And alongside all this there is a new awareness of the dignity and rights of the poor—starting with the right to life, this minimum that is the maximum in Archbishop Romero's phrase, and with it the right to participate in their own history and destiny. God does not want things to go on as they are:

From the depths of the countries that make up Latin America a cry is rising to heaven, growing louder and more alarming all the time. It is the cry of a suffering people who demand justice, freedom, and respect for the basic rights of human beings and peoples [Puebla, 87].

Challenges to Evangelization

I now raise the key question: How to evangelize this kind of world? How to respond to the "muted cry that wells up from millions of human beings, pleading with their pastors for a liberation that is nowhere to be found?" (Puebla, 88). How are we to make ourselves good news for them? To begin with, by what we are. It is the whole of our existence that has to be evangelizing. It is our way of being church, it is the way we live as a religious institute, as Christians, our way of relating to the situation of others, which primarily must be good news today, as in the time of Jesus, for the wretched of the earth, for the poor and oppressed of this world. What we are, our charism and our manner of living it out, must resound today in this world as a cry that proclaims God's mercy and makes those who encounter and nourish their hope through us leap with joy.

The Latin American bishops tell us that "the church must look to Christ when it wants to find out what its evangelizing activity should be like" (Puebla, 1141). Let us recall rapidly what I noted about "the first and greatest evangelizer," applying it to ourselves.

Today the first thing we must do is let ourselves be evangelized, accept the good news of the merciful goodness of God and let ourselves be shaped by it to the point of making our own mercy its manifestation and channel. This means, as we were reminded earlier, conversion to the poor and oppressed, conversion to our brothers and sisters in whose suffering faces we recognize "the suffering features of Christ the Lord, who questions and challenges us" (Puebla, 31). This conversion should apply to the whole church and to ourselves along with it, for— I continue to quote the bishops at Puebla—"not all of us ... have committed ourselves sufficiently to the poor" (see nn. 1134 and 1140). Conversion and reconversion go forward where merciful love continually grows within us, leading us to an ever greater commitment and identification with the poor and their cause.

In a second moment, not so much chronological as dialectical, mercy takes on eyes to see the situation of the poor more profoundly. In our complex, unified, technological world, in which we are conscious that the shocking poverty and suffering of so many are not due to purely natural causes, but are the product of economic, social, and political situations and structures, we must especially look with merciful eyes, but also utilizing any tool that the human and social sciences can offer for interpreting these data coming from reality, so that our looking will not be naive but critical. An example of this new awareness is the Puebla document "Evangelization in the Present and in the Future of Latin America." Part one bears the title "Pastoral Overview of the Reality that is Latin America." No "scientific" approach can replace the "pastoral" in this overview. Mercy remains the basic moving force of evangelization; but in the complexity of our world no uncritical and unenlightened mercy will be able to replace a mercy that in seeking effective response to real needs does not hesitate to also look through the lens of the human and social sciences in order to grasp better the drama of today's world and to be able to discern what is the appropriate word or action.

We should take this pastoral look, however, not from a far-off and protected tower, but from the committed closeness of incarnation. We must approach the situation of those for whom we must become good news. And to approach is to enter into their painful reality, to let ourselves be moved by the brutality of their wounds. It means entering into this culture of poverty, it means suffering the impotence and outcast condition of indigenous people, the despair of drug addicts, the bitterness of mothers who weep for the children who have been snatched away from them. Today we have become aware of this characteristic of true evangelization, and we talk a lot about incarnation, inculturation, insertion, perhaps sometimes without grasping all that this demands of being humbled, of self-emptying. It is a matter of letting the situation and experience of the other speak to us and teach us, patiently, without rushing. In Latin America the initial evangelization took place under the sword; deities and cultures were overturned by force, and the faith was imposed, along with alien religious expressions and

symbols. Today the hierarchy is speaking to us of a new evangelization, one made from within, from the very heart of outcast
cultures, with absolute respect for the identity and freedom of
peoples.

Looking and drawing near in this manner will lead to *compassion*. The other's passion becomes my passion as well, his or
her suffering that hurts in my own flesh — and hence the urgency
to do something to relieve the pain, to eliminate its causes. It
will be a word that consoles, whether announcing or denouncing;
it will be a concrete action that helps break chains, opening
horizons of hope.

There are different ways of drawing near to the situation of
the poor in a Christian manner. We do not have to think that
the approach that enables us to grasp the situation of the other
person and take action must necessarily entail coming close geo-
graphically. In this globalized world with modern means of communication, information flies. Solidarity between communities
enables us to be very well informed and very close to the needs
of the poor and take action about them by strengthening the
evangelizing activity of those who are in fact physically in the
midst of those needs. Today more than ever before, the image
of the body acting through various organs illustrates the poss-
bilities of the church's missionary action. It is organic solidarity
that unleashes the capability of the whole for service.

I can attest firsthand how those Christians, including priests
and religious, who challenge the laws that unjustly prohibit shel-
tering poor displaced foreigners are good news in El Salvador;
I have in mind the sanctuary movement. Or how those men and
women who on the capitol steps struggle for the cause of peace
in Central America or on behalf of Mexican immigrants enhance
the credibility of our preaching of the gospel. No one can be
everywhere or exhaust all the possibilities of evangelizing activity — not even Jesus, who precisely in becoming human flesh
emptied himself and limited himself to one tiny point among
the space-time coordinates of history. It is we who must embody
him concretely and historically in our space and time. But the
church as a whole is sent to "all nations," "to the ends of the
earth," in order to be sacrament of salvation and to announce
and realize the good news of the reign.

Let me continue to illustrate this presentation from the concrete situation of my own Salvadoran church. In order to contribute to the evangelization of El Salvador, there must be an incarnate presence of Christians, priests, men and women religious, missionaries who enter into the reality, history, and culture of this people and right there take up the crucial struggle for life and liberation, volunteers who are ready to carry their witness to the point of martyrdom. Ita, Dorothy, Maura, and Jean, along with Archbishop Romero and so many other martyrs today, continue to be good news for the poor of El Salvador. "As long as there are persons like them who leave everything in order to come to share our life, to suffer and struggle with us, and to die like us and for us, we will have hope, since we know that the God of life has not abandoned us," said an old Salvadoran woman not long ago when the memory of the North American martyrs was being celebrated in a refugee camp.

Solidarity is giving and receiving. The evangelizer is evangelized. Faith, hope, grateful acceptance, the joy with which these persons celebrate life and the courage with which they take on death, the fact that they are as they are—all this in a thousand ways becomes good news that provides the evangelist with meaning, joy, and affection. In them Christ becomes present, more crucified than glorious of course, but he is there and recognizable for those who have eyes to see him. Archbishop Romero used to say, "With this people it is not hard to be a good shepherd." This is the experience of the power that the Lord gives through the ones who, as in the time of Jesus, crowd together in hope around the good news and find there the strength to carry on with their liberating struggle.

Finally, we should not forget that a *good* shepherd is one who gives up his or her life. "Blessed are you when they insult you and persecute you and utter every kind of slander against you because of me. . . . They persecuted the prophets before you in the very same way" (Matt 5:11). The world continues to resist being transformed by the reign of God. The forces of the anti-reign are frighteningly powerful and skillful. They know how to hide evil, distort truth, divide, and when they find it necessary, crush brutally. Archbishop Romero, and the thousands of martyrs who mark the recent history of Latin America, are a convincing proof of that.

In this world we have to pay a price for taking on the cause of the poor, a price that is not a matter of funds but of sharing the same lot and fate, by way of contempt, oppression, and repression. But what is important for our church and for our religious institutes: that the powerful of this world look on us approvingly and support us, or that we be a cry of hope, good news for the despised of the earth? Jesus' words—"Whoever would save his life will lose it, but whoever loses his life for my sake will find it"—are applicable institutionally to the church and to ourselves.

CONCLUSION

At the end of this survey at least three things seem to be clearly established: genuine evangelization can spring only from the root of a mercy that is translated into active solidarity. Whatever form evangelization may take, an inescapable criterion of whether or not it is Christian will always be its ability to be truly "good news" for those crucified within our history. There is a price to pay, the "ransom for the many" (Mark 10:45), for fidelity to the evangelizing mission within a divided and sinful world.

From whatever may be our specific charism within the church, we must let ourselves be questioned and affected by the sufferings of our world and continually, under the guidance of the Spirit, strive to approach that world so we may really be the good news of Christ. An exemplary model of this evangelizing attitude is Mary, type of the evangelizing church. She is the "servant of the Lord," who places herself unconditionally at the liberating service of the God who approaches in goodness and mercy. She gives the Word its human flesh. She hands the Word over to humankind. In her are integrated, without reductionism of any sort, the two essential dimensions of evangelization, that which unites us with the one sending: the Father, from whom all salvation comes, and that which unites us to those to whom our mission directs us: the humble of the earth. Mary is "wholly Christ's and with him . . . wholly the servant of human beings" (Puebla, 294).

The mystery of the visitation is a beautiful compendium of what the church should be. With Christ made flesh in her womb, Mary undergoes the risks of the road to come near to her whose situation has been revealed as a sign. By her being and acting, which out of simplicity radiates the saving kindness she bears in her womb, she becomes good news for Elizabeth, for the Baptist, for these poor persons to whom she in the Magnificat proclaims the joy of a God who does wonders in those who are humble like her, while casting the powerful down from their thrones.

May Mary's example help us to discern the signs of the times, faithful both to the Christ who sends us and to the poor to whom we are sent, and to find the path of evangelization that the modern world needs.

Amando López, S.J.

b. Feb. 6, 1936; d. Nov. 16, 1989
Professor of Theology

Amando got a doctorate in theology at Strasbourg in 1970 and taught that subject at the seminary of San Salvador and the Jesuit universities of both Managua and San Salvador. But his charism was not principally academic. He had instead the gift of giving counsel and building community at every level, and of these Jesuit martyrs (several of whom were workaholics), Amando was probably the one who knew best how to live.

Following his doctoral studies and shortly after arriving in

San Salvador, he had been named rector of the seminary. He had to deal with two years of serious crisis that ended with the Jesuits giving back the management of the seminary to the bishops. The seminarians had grown conscious of unjust social structures in their country and of the church's complicity in them. Certain bishops were unhappy with Amando, though he always felt supported by Arturo Rivera y Damas, the current archbishop.

From there he was named rector of the Jesuit high school in Managua where he had taught as a scholastic. He picked up old friendships—but in quite different circumstances, because the Sandinista revolution that would topple Somoza in 1979 was already underway. He sought out people when he saw them in trouble. He knew how to give his words a touch of humor. People came for his counsel because they knew he was frank, would not curry favor or dispense bromides, and was discreet as a tomb. In this way he picked up a lot of information that in turn helped him give realistic advice to those in danger.

After the Sandinista triumph he became rector of the Central American University in Managua. During this period he was probably the Jesuit who, without actually being a member of the government, had the best relations with the Sandinistas. But the ideological splits that followed the revolution also found their way into the church and the Society of Jesus, and Rome sent him a "visitor" (an official who draws up a special report). Amando took it all with calm, never losing any sleep. But this conflict within the church hurt him deeply, and the upshot was that he left his rector's post.

After a year's sabbatical studying theology in Spain, he returned to Central America, this time to teach theology at the Jesuit university in San Salvador. His lifework became more hidden, without all the connections he enjoyed in Nicaragua. And the Nicaraguans used to complain: "He's not doing anything there. Why did they take him away from us?" As a teacher, his students recall, he was a little boring, although he prepared and knew a lot. He was always open to anyone who might need counseling.

During his last year he had begun to do Sunday pastoral work at Tierra Virgen, a semirural locality on the other side of Soyapango. The affection he lavished on these simple country people, his spontaneous yet well-tuned happiness and his clearly evangelical preaching immediately captivated the whole community. Twenty-five of these friends crossed through perilous combat zones to get to his funeral.

The Reins of Peace

We have seen so much poverty here in El Salvador. And I know that you and the priests here spend a lot of time working with the poor and trying to change that. There are many riches here, yet there is poverty. Why has the country not developed?

We are not really an undeveloped country. We are an *under*-developed country. We are weak in resources, but we could feed ourselves if we needed to. We are really a feudal country. The American economic solution to our problems is good for America, but not for us. El Salvador cannot go on like this. The reason is the immense population and lack of resources. Sixty percent of our people are underemployed. Thirty to forty percent are unemployed. Seven hundred thousand are displaced. A free-market, trickle-down, privatized economy like that of the U.S.A. will not work under these circumstances.

This did not all begin in this decade, of course.

No. Our conflict is a result of this injustice, which has gone on for centuries. So, to put this in terms of an East-West conflict is to miss the point. The more the oppression grows, the more the conflict grows. Today, the more the army grows, the more the guerrillas grow in strength also. The guerrillas are now in all political subdivisions of the country. They are stronger than before the growth in the military.

The country is subsidized by the United States, and has been for many years. The result is that the population is suffering more and more. The state functions only artificially. Without the money that your government sends us, our country would not stand.

But does that mean that El Salvador could not survive without our help?

This interview was conducted in San Salvador in April 1987 by Stan Granot Duncan.

No, it would mean that we would have to survive on our own. The root cause of the fighting here is wealth distribution. If the real wealth of our country were distributed equally, rather than the few having so much more than the many, then there would be enough for all. But the government kills its own people when they cry for bread. They are called "communists" when they organize because they have no food.

It is true, isn't it, that the political killings are down somewhat?

That is true, but because we have gone down from eight thousand to three thousand does not mean that army members are good people. There have been three thousand killings this year confirmed and documented by *Tutela Legal* (the archdiocesan legal aid organization) to have been committed by the government. However, there have been *sixty* confirmed and documented killings by the rebels. The rebels sometimes do terrible things, but they do nothing to us like what the army does. The number of killings may go up and it may go down, but either way it is not according to how good the army is, but how much they feel is necessary to oppress us, reduce us to silence. When they have other more effective ways of controlling us, they use those, and the killing goes down. After killing so many for a while, they can afford to rest for a while now. Killings will go up again as soon as the army determines again that killings are the most effective way of controlling the population, and that committing them is worth the risk of negative publicity from the international press.

What are the chances of the economy's getting better and solving some of the problems causing the unrest?

Probably that would help very little. The wealthy would never on their own allow an economy in which the poor came out of their poverty. President Duarte put out his new economic package recently, and both the right and the left said it was useless.

What did it say?

It was carrot and stick. It had social reform for the poor, but not enough to help them, and privatization and subsidies for the rich, but not enough to make them happy. Nobody wanted it.

The American plan here is to turn the economy over to the oligarchy, but to have small development projects for the poor and propaganda programs about how good it all is for the country, so that the poor will not complain. That plan has not worked. The poor can see through it and the rich do not think it is enough.

Do you think the rebels are getting any outside economic or military help for their fighting?

Probably, but remember that El Salvador is surrounded on all sides by the U.S. army. Either the U.S. army reconnaissance and radar, air force, and navy are all incompetent, or there is not much in arms getting in. If U.S. radar detected great amounts of arms getting into the country, we would hear about it on the media daily. That is the best evidence that not much is coming in.

Where are their weapons coming from?

They do get some of them from outside, but not nearly as much as your government tells you they are getting. Also they get many of them from right here. Most of their weapons are U.S. weapons either sold to them by the Salvadoran army illegally, or captured in battle. And they do not need many supplies. They get much of what they need from the people.

What is it that the rebels are calling for? What do they want?

They want a mixed economy. One that is neither all capitalist nor all socialist. And they want a new military, with the most brutal elements in it purged from it and with the FMLN integrated into it.

Would there be a communist state here if the rebels won?

Maybe, but you must see a difference between a communist economy and Russian bases. In my opinion the best thing for the United States is for Latin America to have a socialist government, nonaligned, with no Soviet bases. The previous U.S. ambassador in Managua told me when I was there that he wished that El Salvador had the Sandinista form of government.

What is the relation of the church to the poor?

The church never advocates revolution, but there is much coincidence between the church's commitments to the poor and the growth of the struggles that have now become part of the war. Often the fighters were taught originally by priests about justice and that God is for the poor. When they saw their government imposing its will to keep the will of God from the people, they became fighters. Many of them did not want to fight—many still do not want to fight. But they believed what the church taught about the fair distribution of wealth, of the dignity of all persons. And they began fighting for that.

We used to have two newspapers that were moderate, more open. They were both bombed by the army, and their journalists killed. There were many priests here who once stood with the people who are dead or are now in hiding. The people see that and they are angry. They take up arms to right the wrongs that are being done to them.

Why have you not advocated fighting also?

We believe in some of the goals of the FMLN, but I cannot fight and I cannot tell others to take up arms to fight. But that does not mean that we do not understand the position of those who do. We sometimes talk of leaving, also. But our hope is not in leaving, it is here. If I leave, the crisis will stay. Here I may be able to effect change.

We try to work with the government. To let them know that the real route to peace lies with them, not the rebels. We try to tell the United States embassy that if they would not supply the military aid, the Salvadoran government would listen more sensibly to what the people are saying. We try to keep close ties to the government because we believe that they hold the reins of peace.

～ 6 ～

Segundo Montes, S.J.

b. May 15, 1933; d. Nov. 16, 1989
Superior of the Community

We knew Segundo as fiery-spirited from the moment we met him in the novitiate. He kicked the soccer ball with all his might, rocketing it into the neighborhood to break rooftiles. Afterward would come "fraternal correction," which Segundo accepted with humility and without resentment. But it cost him, because he was so ardent. Next recreation period he would break more tiles.

He was practical. He loved to take things apart and put them back together. On the night of his death, he was going around the new house, connecting up the telephone. In his early years he taught physics. The exact sciences always held an attraction for him, and the sociological writings of his later years were always accompanied by statistics.

He was forceful in expression, even exaggerated, and judgments on antagonists were strong. Anyone hearing him on such people might suppose them quite irredeemable, but those who knew Segundo also knew of his compassion and, indeed, his knack for being a reconciler. This latter was recognized in his often being named a community leader.

In the 1970s he had realized he could serve El Salvador better as a social analyst than as a physicist, so he studied anthropology in Madrid, where he got a degree with honors in 1978. He arrived back in Central America with his characteristic energy to teach sociology at the Central American University and to head up the department of sociology and political science. With the help of students he launched surveys in the countryside and the city. Of the six Jesuit martyrs, he was the one who knew El Salvador best from direct personal experience. He wrote about landholdings and social classes, about refugees and human rights. He filled page after page. He wrote easily and gracefully, though not much given to the study of letters as such.

He became director of the Human Rights Institute and began to go to meetings abroad, where he presented the results of his study of refugees and human rights, principally. He was aware, therefore, that he might be a marked man. His last trip, at the beginning of November, was to Washington, D.C., where he was honored by CARECEN (which in Spanish means "they need"), an organization that aids refugees, and by the Washington Office on Latin America (WOLA), for his refugee and human-rights work.

He never lost touch with the people. Every weekend he said Mass in a poor neighborhood of Santa Tecla. They loved him there because he was so simple in his personal dealings. To this community he would narrate his experiences in the even poorer refugee resettlements, and they tell how he could make them "feel like worms," describing how a refugee family would give him the one egg they had for the whole family. He evangelized the poor with the example of those who were even poorer. He told them how he had celebrated Mass under gunfire in Perquin, where he had spent Holy Week a couple of years ago.

The people recall his face especially—his Viking beard and fiery cheeks, enough to put the fear of God into anyone. At the university they had nicknamed him Zeus. But little children did not fear him. They liked to put their faces right up against his. And in that face the most outstanding feature were his eyes, which deep down had a trace of sadness and seemed on the watch for God, eyes that looked surprised when he received a gift. Then they would fill with tears, and he would say with a few, abrupt words: "Thanks, I don't deserve it."

God's Grace Does Not Leave

What is your assessment of the general human rights condition in El Salvador right now?

It improved in some ways for a few years. The terrible mass killings got more selective, and fewer in numbers. The military has allowed a "democratic space" to open up so that opposition parties will come back to the country and legitimize the government. But that appears to be changing. Things appear to be going down hill.

Why is that?

The country is much more unstable than it used to be. Things could blow up at any time and under the surface they are blowing up right now. Some people believe the election victory of the ARENA party (the party of the far right) is a green light, that they no longer need to follow the rule of law.

Laws like what?

Laws like those against detaining persons for several days without accusing them of anything, or laws against executing suspects in their homes instead of bringing them to trial. When your government defends abuses of freedom as ways to fight communism, the fringes get legitimized. Their behavior comes to be considered the center. They begin to think of themselves as patriots for killing "terrorists." Adolfo Blandón has proposed new antiterrorist legislation for the National Assembly, which will make nearly all of us fall into the category of terrorists. Even friends and acquaintances of terrorists can be detained without charge. If laws like those are passed, then it will legalize the repression, and killing campesinos will become a legal part of "democracy."

Do you see any possibility of things getting any better here at all, in terms of human rights abuses?

This interview with Stan Granot Duncan took place in April 1988.

If you look at our history, you see that there is a reduction of numbers. But, again, much of that is related to the army's getting smarter about whom it oppresses and how it oppresses. With a history of killing our population at random, now they can terrorize persons and threaten them, and the threats are taken seriously, because the population knows that the army really can do it. Also, you have to remember that for a time there were simply fewer persons to kill. The Treasury Police and the death squads, which are clearly related to the government, took much of the strength out of the popular movements in the early 1980s by killing and having so many persons disappear. It has taken time for new ones to get the courage to replace them. There were many more mouths here in those days, when a thousand or fifteen hundred persons per month were being killed or were disappearing. You cannot continue that level of killing of innocent persons indefinitely. There are not that many to kill.

Do you think that ARENA will back a strong war if it takes control of the presidency (which it did in the elections of March 1989)?

That depends a lot on how far the United States is willing to back them. They do not appear to have much support outside the United States. Many countries consider ARENA to be a terrorist organization. At the same time, the [U.S.] embassy here is calling them "democrats." If Congress believes that, ARENA will grow strong and confident, and perhaps conduct an even more repressive war. Also, when you speak of any government in El Salvador, you must truly speak of the military high command first. It is not clear yet how much power the next government will be allowed to have. Duarte had almost none. That was in part because the armed forces and the far right perceived the goals of the Christian Democratic Party as being different from its own. ARENA begins with its goals already being very similar to those of the military. Many military leaders are also leaders of the ARENA party. But the question then is, will a new civilian ARENA president actually control this country, or will he just appear to be in control because his goals and those of the most repressive elements of the military are the same?

What about restrictions on freedom of the press?

Most of our press has never felt free—at least as you would know it. However, because of the "democratic opening" some of them have been covering things recently that they never would have before. If the press were to be repressed again, the first place we would see it would be in the rural places, like Chalatenango, where there is much fighting and where the army would not want information to get out.

What about death squad activity? How much evidence is there that they are on the rise again?

We are beginning to see more effects of torture in the killings. It looks like they are rising again. There are more bodies being dumped at the Puerto de Diablo and other places. That is a trademark of their work. When troops are in uniform, they are less inclined to torture the campesinos or students or union workers whom they kill or capture. It can be traced back to them more easily. When they work in one of the death squads, without uniforms, they feel much more free to torture. For that reason, the increase in torture tells us that there may be an increase in the work of the death squads.

That style is back, but we don't know anything about their structures. We think that they have been restructured, but we don't know. Before you leave El Salvador, ask some of the foreign journalists. Some of them have been looking into the military's restructure of the death squads. They can tell you more about that.

Are you personally ever threatened here? You or others on your staff?

Oh, yes. It comes and goes. I have not received a death threat for some months, but they will come again soon, I am certain.

Have you ever been so frightened that you would want to leave the country?

Yes, back in the early 1980s, when the killing of priests was so terrible, I thought of that. Several of us here at the university talked about leaving, of seeking freedom in the United States, or Spain. But we decided—there is a saying—how can we be really free if our brothers and sisters are not free? This is my country and these people are my people. We here are not just teachers and social scientists. We are also parish priests, and the people need to have the church stay with them in these terrible times—the rich as well as the poor. The rich need to hear from us, just as do the poor. God's grace does not leave, so neither can we.

～ 7 ～

Joaquin López y López, S.J.

"Lolo"
b. Aug. 16, 1918; d. Nov. 16, 1989
National Director, "Fe y Alegría"

"Lolo" (López y López) is the only one of the six who
belonged to a different generation. He was the oldest and the
only native Salvadoran. It seems the murderers separated him
from the others. Not only did they put him in a room, but they
did not blast his brains out, as they did with the other priests.

His family were from Santa Ana, rich people, owners of coffee plantations and a famous dairy. But he left that at an early

age, finishing high school in a minor seminary. Throughout his life he was exemplary in his self-denial and fondness for secondhand things — never a trace of luxury. Though he handled a lot of money in his day, none of it ever stuck to him. Friends from his own background helped him in works as important as starting up the Central American University, but he kept his independence. He spent his entire apostolic life in El Salvador.

He was a man of few words, not always audible or well-pronounced. He seemed at times to regret what he was saying. He was timid, without the charism of a university professor. But what an impresario of education at the more popular level! The harbinger of what would become *Fe y Alegría* ("Faith and Joy"), the movement he directed, could be seen in the catechism classes in poor neighborhoods that he organized from the boarding school where he worked. He knew how to motivate students from various schools to spend part of their weekend among the needy.

This knack for organizing and networking helped him in 1964 to start a campaign to found the Central American University. He remembered those years with pleasure. It was one of the few subjects on which he was expansive. Starting with a national federation of parents, he organized from the high school a fund drive and popular support for the legal chartering of a private university, seen in those days as a non-Marxist alternative. He stayed on at the university for only a few years, since his talents lay elsewhere. But for many years he signed documents as secretary of the faculty. Father Ellacuría (the rector) was eager that Lolo form part of the university community when it was reorganized in 1988, precisely because of the part he played in its beginning and the bonds of affection that joined him to it. So it was no mere chance that the blow aimed at the Jesuits of Central American University struck him down, too.

Fe y Alegría, with its 13 schools, 12 workshops and 8,000 students, with its two clinics and their 50,000 clients, was for him an immediate response to one of El Salvador's most serious problems, the lack of education. He did not deny the importance of "structural change," but he thought the needs of the people needed looking after today. He could come across as caught up in the immediate, putting himself in debt during the school term, placing his trust in God—and the big raffle at the end of the year. Before closing any schools, when income was down, again and again he would try his raffles, which came through for him despite the economic crisis.

Lolo was a man already condemned—not by any death squad, but by prostate cancer. He did not know how long he had. Meanwhile he kept working tirelessly, until, without his suspecting it would be this way, the enemies of his poor people did the Reaper's business.

～ 8 ～

Elba and Celina Ramos

Mother and Daughter
b. Mar. 5, 1947, and Feb. 27, 1973
d. Nov. 16, 1989

Elba was born in Santiago Maria. Her mother, Santos, sold fruit, and her father, whose name does not appear on the birth certificate, was a plantation boss. Around 1967 Elba met the man with whom she would live the rest of her life in a common-law marriage. He had been working as an overseer at a plantation in Santa Tecla. She had been working as a domestic in San Salvador, and when she asked permission to do some coffee-picking, she ended up in her future husband's section.

She stopped working when they set up their home. At that time they were living on the land of Ernesto Liebes, who gave them economic help, but he died in one of the first of the violent kidnappings, so they left in 1970. They moved to Jayaque, where her husband looked after someone else's farm and also grew some corn and beans, with which Elba gave him a hand. It was there that Celina was born. She was the third child, really, for Elba had already had two babies, the first a little boy who was stillborn and the second another boy who died shortly after birth. After Celina, another boy arrived in 1976, and he is still alive.

Also in 1976, looking for a better life, they moved to Acujutla. They had to leave in 1979 because of violence that destroyed the husband's source of work. Then they moved back to Santa Tecla, where they rented a little house that was essentially a box with a dirt floor and a curtain down the middle. He got work as gardener for a rich gentleman who left the country in 1985 because of land reform, whereupon he got work as a neighborhood night watchman.

That same year Elba started working for the Jesuits at the new theologate, cooking and cleaning. She was there from the start, and it was through Elba that her husband later got work as a guard at the Jesuit university. Father Amando López (who was also murdered Nov. 16) knew Elba from the theologate and liked her. He had the idea that a small family was needed for the guardhouse and suggested Elba and her husband, who came to work at the university in July of 1989. The family of four did not move into the guardhouse till a few weeks later. Elba kept on working at the theologate, a 15-minute walk away, and in fact she never worked for the Jesuits at the university. Her husband was the guard at a main gate of the university, which opened onto the area where the Jesuit residence was located.

As for Celina, by 1989 she was in the first year of a high school commercial course. She had received a scholarship along with two companions from her primary school, and every so often she had to show her marks to the lawyer who had given them the scholarship. The need to concentrate on studies had led her to give up basketball and band, a sacrifice for someone so active. She also interrupted her work as a catechist. Even so, she seems to have been hard-pressed because she left two subjects incomplete. She had had a boyfriend since she was 14. He too liked basketball and was on his school team. They had thought they might get married soon, depending on what Elba said. Elba used to advise him and show him a lot of affection, and he planned to break the news to her in December.

At the theologate they remember Elba as an exceptional person: loyal, discreet, intuitive in spotting signs of distress in another's face. Then she would speak poetically, using metaphors, giving advice to the person she thought was down. She was sensitive to the needs of others, and on the day before she was killed she washed her best dress (a black one with a pink flower design) for a woman who had taken refuge in the theologate from the bombing. She was going to give it to her the next day.

That Wednesday, Nov. 15, when Elba walked up to the theologate, she brought a change of clothes in case she couldn't get back and had to sleep there. Since the preceding Sunday, the mother and daughter had not slept in the guardhouse, because on Saturday the guerrillas had set off a bomb at the gate. Amando López had told them they would be safer in the Jesuit residence. Then, that Wednesday, the two of them managed to get back in the evening from the theologate to the Jesuit residence. They even cooked supper for the Jesuits.

The theologians had told Elba to stay up there, but she did not want to be away from her husband. She wanted to make sure he got his supper. This loyalty called her to her death. Her husband, who spent the night in the guardhouse, was saved. Her little boy, who on Saturday had gone with cousins to Acajutla, was also saved.

PART III

The Jesuits
and
the University

The Task of a Christian University

Ignacio Ellacuría, S.J.

It is a great honor for me, and a gesture of solidarity and support for the Universidad Centroamericana José Simeón Cañas, that the University of Santa Clara has decided to confer upon me this honorary degree.

I am sure you intend primarily not to single out my intellectual activity but to commend the academic and social work which our university has conducted for over seventeen years. It is work oriented, obviously, on behalf of our Salvadoran culture, but above all on behalf of a people who, oppressed by structural injustices, struggle for their self-determination, people often without liberty or human rights.

At present, as you know, the United States represents the major political force in Central America — and certainly in El Salvador. The social and political destiny of El Salvador, whether we like it or not, depends to a large extent on the U.S. government. It is therefore of the utmost importance that the United States carry out an informed and just foreign policy in Central America. It must take into consideration the real interests of the American people; but, more important for us, it must

---

This talk was delivered at graduation exercises at the Jesuit-run University of Santa Clara in California on June 12, 1982.

correspond to the principles of political ethics and to the needs of a people suffering misery and oppression not because of their fault or indolence, but because of a chain of historical events for which they cannot be held responsible.

Some North American congressmen are looking for just solutions for Salvadorans, though such solutions are, admittedly, difficult and risky. Some churches and religious groups such as the Catholic bishops of the United States have exerted themselves on our behalf and have pressed the present administration not to intensify our conflicts through military reinforcement but to facilitate a just, negotiated solution.

American universities have an important part to play in order to ensure that the unavoidable presence of the United States in Central America be sensitive and just, especially those universities that are inspired by the desire to make present among us all the kingdom of God.

Obviously, our university is also engaged in this task. We bear the name of a Salvadoran priest, José Simeón Cañas, who as a congressman in the Constitutional Assembly advocated and obtained in 1824 the abolition of slavery in Central America. He addressed these words to the assembly:

I come crawling, and if I were dying, dying I would come to make a request for humanity. I beg before anything else that our slaves be declared free citizens. This is the order of justice: that the deprived be restored to the possession of their goods, and no good is more valuable than liberty. We all know that our brothers have been violently deprived of their freedom, that they grieve in servitude, sighing for a hand to break the iron chains of slavery. The nation has declared itself free; so then must all the people be free.

Abraham Lincoln signed the Emancipation Proclamation in 1863, forty years after José Simeón Cañas, who was a priest, a scholar and a politician, obtained emancipation for the slaves of Central America.

Our university works in that same spirit of liberation today. Let me say a word about how we understand ourselves so that you can comprehend and support us more responsibly.

There are two aspects to a university. The first and most evident is that it has to do with culture, with knowledge, the use of the intellect. The second, not so evident, is that it must be concerned with the social reality—precisely because a university is inescapably a social force: it must transform and enlighten the society in which it lives. But how does it do that? How does it transform the social reality of which it is a part?

There is no abstract and consistent answer here. A university cannot always and in every place be the same. We should always look at our own peculiar historical reality. For us in El Salvador the historical reality is that we are a part of the Third World, which is itself the major portion of humankind. Unfortunately, the Third World is characterized more by oppression than by liberty, by injustice than justice, by terrible poverty rather than by abundance. . . .

What does a university do, immersed in this reality? Transform it? Yes. Do everything possible so that liberty is victorious over oppression, justice over injustice, love over hate? Yes. Without this overall commitment, we would not be a university, and even less so would we be a Catholic university.

But how is this done? The university must carry out this general commitment with the means uniquely at its disposal: we as an intellectual community must analyze causes; use imagination and creativity together to discover remedies; communicate to our constituencies a consciousness that inspires the freedom of self-determination; educate professionals with a conscience, who will be the immediate instruments of such a transformation; and continually hone an educational institution that is academically excellent and ethically oriented.

How does a university shape itself, or come to understand itself and its social obligations?

Liberation theology has emphasized what the preferential option for the poor means in authentic Christianity. Such an option constitutes an essential part of Christian life—and also a historic obligation. The poor embody Christ in a special way; they mirror for us his message of revelation, salvation, and conversion. And they are also a universal historical reality.

Reason and faith merge, therefore, in confronting the reality of the poor. Reason must open its eyes to the fact of suffering.

Faith, which is sometimes scandalous to those without it, sees in the weak of this world the triumph of God, for we see in the poor what salvation must mean and the conversion to which we are called.

A Christian university must take into account the gospel preference for the poor. This does not mean that only the poor study at the university; it does not mean that the university should abdicate its mission of academic excellence — excellence needed in order to solve complex social problems. It does mean that the university should be present intellectually where it is needed: to provide science for those who have no science; to provide skills for the unskilled; to be a voice for those who have no voice; to give intellectual support for those who do not possess the academic qualifications to promote and legitimate their rights.

We have attempted to do this. In a modest way, we have made a contribution through our research and publications, and a few men have left more lucrative positions to work in the university for the people.

We have been thanked and supported in our efforts. We have also been severely persecuted. From 1976 to 1980, our campus was bombed ten times; we have been blocked, raided by military groups, and threatened with the termination of all financial aid. Dozens of students and teachers have had to flee the country in exile; a student was shot to death by police who entered the campus. Our history has been that of our nation.

But we have also been encouraged by the words of Archbishop Romero — himself soon to be murdered — who said, while we were burying an assassinated priest, that something would be wrong in our church if no priest lay next to so many of his assassinated brothers and sisters. If the university had not suffered, we would not have performed our duty. In a world where injustice reigns, a university that fights for justice must necessarily be persecuted.

I should like to think — and this is the meaning I give to this honorary degree — that you understand our efforts, our mission, something of the tragic reality of El Salvador.

And how do you help us? That is not for me to say. Only open your human heart, your Christian heart, and ask yourselves the three questions Ignatius of Loyola put to himself as he stood in front of a crucified world: What have I done for Christ in this world? What am I doing now? And above all, what should I do? The answers lie both in your academic responsibility and in your personal responsibility. . . .

To all of you, many thanks.

∼ 10 ∼

The University's Christian Inspiration

Jon Sobrino, S.J.

To clarify the future of the university from the perspective of theology and its requirements, it is worthwhile turning to something that precedes theology and the university: the fundamental principles of Christian faith. These principles, respecting the particular nature of theology and the university, are the ones that can provide guidance, empowerment, and critique for both, shedding light on their interrelationship as well. To state it clearly from the outset, I think that a Christian university is one that places itself at the service of the kingdom of God from an option for the poor. This service must be done *as* a university, and even by means of a university's particular nature.

THE PROBLEM OF THE CHRISTIAN INSPIRATION OF A UNIVERSITY

Personally, I believe in the possibility and efficacy of a university with Christian inspiration, but must also say that recent university history does not make this obvious. Therefore, in

This essay was presented on June 4, 1987, at the University of Deusto, Bilbao, during the University's centenary celebration. It was published in *Estudios Centroamericanas* (no. 468, October 1987).

order not to fall into mere conceptualism or idealism, an analysis must be made as well of the problems universities face in living out their Christian inspiration. Such an analysis is necessary so that, in thinking of the future, this shadow-side of universities may be effectively overcome.

As regards methodology, the possibility must be admitted at the outset that a university can vitiate its Christian inspiration, that concupiscence and the sinfulness inherent in everything human may also be active in a university. This possibility, which is always to be kept in mind in analyzing individuals and social groups, including the church—which is both "saint and sinner"—must be admitted, too, where the university is concerned, for there is nothing in a university that would remove it from this condition. In other words, a university can be Christian, a-Christian, or even anti-Christian, and this not only in some of its members or in some of its sectors, but in the university as such. It would be an illusion to think that the university cannot be an instrument of the antikingdom and of sin (although it can and ought to be an instrument of the kingdom and of grace), or that it does not need to ask pardon of society, although, with modesty, it can also be open to society's gratitude.

This more pessimistic methodological consideration is not made purely a priori. Without falling into unjust anachronisms, it cannot be overlooked that Christian universities have left much to be desired in their response to the world and have even contributed to strengthening the antikingdom. Today's world as a whole, the Third World certainly, but also with analogies in other worlds, is a world of sin, in which falsehood prevails over truth, oppression over justice, repression over freedom and—in words that are, unfortunately, not at all rhetorical—death over life. In this real world, the university has been invited and required to incarnate itself in one reality or another, placing its social weight on behalf of one or the other. And this, in my judgment, provides the fundamental criterion for verifying whether or not and to what extent Christian inspiration has been operative in a university.

Far too frequently Christian universities have not questioned a society's unjust structures, or used their social weight to denounce them, or have they made central to their work the research and planning of new models for society. As a matter of fact, by producing professional persons who, in most cases, have served to support unjust systems, Christian universities have effectively supported the evils of today's world.

In the political realm, universities have, by their silence or by their explicit support, not hindered, much less stood in opposition to, inhumane practices that are grave violations of freedom and the most fundamental human rights. In Latin America, Christian universities have not distinguished themselves by their opposition to the dictatorships and national security regimes so much condemned later by everyone, once they have fallen. It cannot be said that universities have dared to run institutional risks in order to face up as universities to repressive regimes.

In the religious-ecclesial realm, evaluation can be more nuanced. But not infrequently universities have lined up with ecclesiastical forces that are conservative or even reactionary, distancing themselves from the church's more open and gospel forces. Their contribution to the religious-ecclesial realm, and through this to life in society, has left much to be desired.

This is not everything that Christian universities have done, but it is a very important part of what they have done. To overlook it too easily, not to confront this shadow-side of the university, would in no way help to clarify its Christian inspiration.

These facts seem to me undeniable, but it is more important to ask ourselves why, or what, there is in the university situation that makes it possible and even tends to justify it. In my opinion, there are two reasons for this. The first is the tendency toward a selective incarnation in society; and the second, an unreflective appeal to the autonomy of university learning.

Whether by design or not, the university is incarnated in social reality; but because it represents in itself a power — intellectual power — and because it needs abundant resources for its subsistence and growth, it has the tendency to situate itself in the world of power: economic, political, or ecclesiastical power, depending on the case. That world, insofar as it is a locus of power, is always a temptation; it conditions the university's existence and the determination and direction of what it seeks to do. It imbues university decisions with extreme caution when these powers are in any way threatened, thus endangering the university itself. But the most important thing is that this incarnation amid power tends to distance the university from social reality as lived by the poorest and most marginalized. Incarnation in a world of power leads to a disincarnation from the social world of the majority and, in a Christian sense, from the social world most demanded by faith and most apt for the living out of Christian inspiration. This may result in a manner of working and presenting itself to the world that is out of harmony with gospel ideals, but above all results in a distancing from the world on the underside of history, where the demands of the kingdom of God are best understood.

An unreflective appeal to the autonomy of university learning is also dangerous. It is a necessary appeal in the face of any kind of unwarranted pressure, but a dangerous appeal if by it university learning should feign ignorance of social reality and if university knowledge should cease to critique itself. The human person seeks truth through reason, but not through reason alone. The sociology of knowledge teaches us that there is always interest prior to knowledge.

Epistemology demonstrates that to intelligence belongs not only the weight of establishing and giving meaning to reality, but also its ethical and practical dimensions. In the words of Ignacio Ellacuría, "to study a situation" is indissolubly linked with "accepting the burden of that situation" and "becoming responsible for the situation." Reason is not immune from the ethical and the practical; and from the point of view of revelation, it is not even immune from concupiscence and sinfulness. Truth may be manipulated, not merely attained, by wickedness and injustice (Romans 1:18).

Knowledge, in other words, can respond to different interests, consciously or unconsciously, and the inevitable need to verify which interests are served by knowledge does not disappear by any appeal to its autonomy. Knowledge can be reduced to the noetic moment itself, thereby intentionally evading ethical and practical responsibility; knowledge can discover and demonstrate reality but also cover it over and suppress it. A university, like any other institution, can serve one group of interests or another, can serve reality or abandon it to its misery, can denounce or justify it. And this ambiguity is typical of the university in the name of its specific instrumentality: knowledge.

The Christian character of a university is not, therefore, evident by the mere fact that a particular university is called Christian. In view of recent history—and certainly from the Third World—the university's Christian character is rather questionable. If there can and should be a Christian university, then it should be demonstrated what conditions permit the fostering of what is Christian and the overcoming or minimizing of negative by-products.

Before speaking of the Christian principles that can guide a university and be operative in a university situation, it is important to analyze some university activities that can seem to be a justification of a Christian university. These activities are or can be good in themselves, but I see them as insufficient, for both theoretical and historical reasons, in light of the negative by-products they produce.

In the first place, the educational dimension of a university is not a sufficient justification. The horizon and finality of a university, as we shall see, is social reality as such. The education and formation of individuals from that horizon and to that end is important in itself: but if there is a concentration on that and it serves to hide the primary horizon and finality, it is dangerous. It is good to promote education, even of just a few, but it is dangerous if that leads to a concern for the education of those few and only of them. The problem is not one of numbers, but rather of horizon; of whether, consciously or unconsciously, the educational values to be promoted are determined from the few rather than from the many, or even against the many. Education, as professional education, is a still weaker justification because, with rare exceptions, university graduates reinforce the social systems that do not benefit the poor majorities and, in the Third World, are against the majorities, with resources that, in the final analysis, come from the majorities.

In the second place, the Christian formation of university members, particularly the students, is also not sufficient justification. Besides the intrinsic difficulty of managing to respond to them in any major way and of making the student body an important social force of Christian inspiration, the university is only accidentally a place of pastoral activity. The Christian character of a university is not measured by religious practices, but rather by service to a more human configuration of society—through what is Christian—and by service to the configuration of a people of God as leaven for the kingdom of God in society. No less is it sufficient justification in secularized societies that a specific university offer a secure place in which faith can still be maintained. Although it may be a noble task, this too is not what the university is specifically about, and it is dangerous if these religious/pastoral activities—often converted into islands within the university—should offer an excuse for not carrying out other more specifically university-related Christian tasks.In the third place, it is also not sufficient justification that the university be a place of theological production. It is such, undoubtedly, and it does offer great advantages for this: the rigorous exercise of theological reasoning, interdisciplinary studies—if they are really carried out—and an empowering, mutual criticism with other fields of knowledge. From this point of view, the university offers the possibility of a scientific theology more open to truth and less subject to vested interests: it offers the possibility of "declericalizing" theology. But it also offers the temptation of disconnecting theology from its real roots in history and in the people of God, of "depopularizing" theology. This is dangerous, not because theology, its rigor, and its methods, may be different from the living out and self-reflection of faith among the poor— which is evident and necessary—but rather because it may distance theology from the real substance of faith and the real hopes of the poor, and lead theology to believe that it does not need them. That a university has theological production is important; but this does not automatically transform it into a Christian university, until we see what kind of theology is produced and whether the fact that it is done at a university helps it to be a more Christian theology.

Finally, it is also not sufficient justification that a university, through its school of theology, become a defender of ecclesiastical orthodoxy. It is important that once a Christian university exists, it relate to orthodoxy, clarifying and bringing out the potential of the real truth in orthodoxy and defending it, even though it is complicated to determine precisely in what this defense consists and what will be the best way to defend it. But the finality of a Christian university does not lie formally in the defense of a truth accepted a priori, but rather in making society grow in the direction of the kingdom of God through whatever is true in the tradition and through the continuing clarification of that truth so that it may become fruitful.

CHRISTIAN PRINCIPLES THAT INSPIRE A UNIVERSITY

From this historical consideration, I want to mention some Christian principles that, of their nature, offer a better hope of overcoming the limitations and negative tendencies of a university and of inspiring in a positive way its Christian task. These are principles drawn from faith, although interpreted by a theology—which may make them a matter for discussion. They are principles that should be applied in history according to times and situations, according to which there can be discussion as to how and whether they can be applied. But they are suggested because they have given birth to important university and Christian realities.

The first principle is the kingdom of God as horizon to be kept in mind and as finality for a Christian university. As a horizon, the kingdom of God points to a new world, which, in turn, makes reference to the reality of an old world. What this old world may be, what is the reality of the world in which we live, is the first question posed by the kingdom of God. In general, it is not difficult to admit that the world as such is in crisis: a crisis of reality, of nuclear and ecological threats, and a crisis of meaning, of human meaning and the meaning of faith. But the major crisis is that of life itself. For those of us who live in the Third World, this crisis is a fact of daily experience, and any scientific analysis of society verifies it. At the close of the century, a third of Latin America's population, about one hundred seventy million human beings, will be almost unable to reach a subsistence level, will be subject to biological poverty, which is to say, the inability to satisfy their basic vital needs. The more universal and blatant reality is that of poverty, defined in the Third World as a real nearness to death, to the slow death imposed by unjust and oppressive economic structures—Medellín calls it "institutionalized violence"—and to sudden and violent death, when repression or the wars spawned by poverty produce numerous victims. From this vantage point, other crises and other poverties will need to be understood analogically, but here is the prime analogue. In Christian terms, the world has not managed to become the creation God wanted, but rather, on the contrary, is a world of death, is sin.

This is no novelty in the history of humanity. The Old Testament and Jesus of Nazareth saw the world in this way and amid this reality proclaimed the kingdom of God as God's response to the sin of the world. With this proclamation it is affirmed above all that, despite all appearances, there can be hope. There is good news and a meaning to history, but understood not primarily as the meaning of individuals who already have their lives guaranteed; rather as the meaning of history felt by whole peoples and the majorities of humanity.

In the second place, the proclamation of the kingdom of God is a practical demand to make it happen, to create history according to the good news proclaimed, to transform history. From the original compassion that the real world should produce, we must posit signs that the kingdom is possible and, above all, transform oppressive structures so that new ones may guarantee life and not death.

Finally, the kingdom of God is utopia: it moves toward developments that are ever broader and fuller, toward greater freedom and improved culture, toward more humanization and a more complete openness to God. But this utopia should develop from the necessary minimum: from a just life for the poor majorities that can make community possible. Without a just life, history itself is deprived of meaning; and without community, human lives lack meaning.

That kingdom of God is the horizon and finality of all Christian activity, both personal and institutional, as it is also of a university. The kingdom demands certain conditions of the university and offers it as well some possibilities. The kingdom demands above all that the university understand itself explicitly as one of the social forces through which the kingdom is or is not being built up, without the university's appealing subtly or grossly to the autonomy of learning in order to feign ignorance of its intrinsic social dimension in shaping the kingdom. It demands that the university seek its center outside itself—decentering is a Christian demand not only on individuals but also on institutions—in order that they place themselves at the service of the kingdom and not of themselves. It demands that a university as a whole reach out to society in order to lead it toward the kingdom, in such a way that specifically university activities—research and teaching—be transformed into a social project; it demands that the university project signs and structures of the kingdom, and that this projection be not merely something drawn from the facts of research and teaching—whether for or against the kingdom—but something explicitly sought, cultivated, and verified. It also demands that the university take on the sin of the anti-kingdom, for kingdom and antikingdom are not coequal historical possibilities. On the contrary, the former should be proclaimed and carried out in and against the latter. We must be clear about the fact that the university does not operate in a neutral world, but rather in a world fraught with antikingdom, which is seeking actively to place the university at its service, and it reacts against the university when the latter denounces and unmasks it and seeks to replace it with the kingdom. It would be an illusion to think that the university cannot or should not be subject to attacks and persecutions; and persecution by the powerful becomes an important principle of verification later as to whether a university has had or has lacked a Christian inspiration.

But the kingdom of God also offers possibilities to the university. It orients the basic hypotheses of the university as a whole: what is the fundamental sin to be denounced and eradicated, what is the direction that should determine all the university's functions and activities. The kingdom facilitates for the university a unified understanding of its diverse functions—research, teaching, and social projects—in such a way that these do not turn into conflicting dimensions but rather converge toward a single goal. The kingdom encourages the investigation of reality according to its resemblance to or dissemblance from the kingdom; communication through teaching of what has been researched and discovered; projecting it in society and changing it according to what has been researched.

The kingdom of God can also generate a mystique in the

university as a whole and in its members. It offers above all a sense of reality, that the university is part of this world, with its joys and sorrows, that it is coresponsible with and not separate from the rest of humanity. It offers dignity, not in the worldly sense of praise and prestige, but in the sense of serving human life. It offers reconciliation with, not distance from, other human beings. In a Christian sense, it offers the meaning and joy of following Jesus in a university.

In this way, the university can also unify two problems that in some places appear quite distinct: the problem of the practical transformation of society and the problem of contextual meaning. Because of historical conditioning in some places, one or another problem may be more emphasized. But it can be asked whether one—not the only—cause of contextual meaninglessness may not lie in a double disconnectedness: that of the individual with respect to humanity, and that of the meaning of one's own life with respect to the reality itself of life. To orient oneself by the kingdom of God may be one form, certainly not a mechanical one, of reconciling the individual with humanity and thus, the meaning of life with life itself. In this way the university can be, not only a transforming social force, but also a locus of meaning.

The second principle is the option for the poor. Theoretically, the kingdom of God can be promoted in diverse ways, but from a faith perspective it should be carried out from an option for the poor. This option, in fact, is not a specifically Christian thing, but Christian faith elevates it to something of a right. In one sense, it has a more specifically Christian logic than the kingdom of God. The reality and even the terminology of the option for the poor is not often reflected upon theoretically in the First World—even though the extraordinary synod in Rome has universalized it—and it may baffle some persons as a guiding principle for a university. The reason may be that it is considered as and reduced to a purely pastoral ecclesial topic foreign to the university; and the substantial partiality of the option for the poor seems to be a threat to the universality of the university.

But the option for the poor is not reduced to a pastoral option, nor, even though it is specific, does it deny universality. The option for the poor, before becoming concretized in pastoral forms of ecclesial activity, is a hermeneutical principle, a preunderstanding consciously adopted, a hypothesis, if you will (J. L. Segundo), in order to observe and analyze reality and act accordingly; and it is a conviction—present in Christian faith and confirmed historically by many—that from this perspective one can observe reality better and more thoroughly, and act more effectively to improve reality. The option for the poor, then, is something that has to do theologically and anthropologically with every human being at every level of their reality—whether they know it or not; it is no mere regional and pastoral entity. Nor is it, on the other hand, a threat to the university: because, empirically, humanity in general is quantitatively poor; but more important yet, because the option for the poor does not mean to focus on a part of the whole in order to ignore the rest, but rather to reach out to the whole from one part.

What the option for the poor demands and makes possible at a university is a place of incarnation insofar as the university is a social force, and a specific light for its own learning. Incarnation—or better, adequate incarnation—is something essential in Christianity, and not merely a problem to be resolved at the intentional level, for incarnation supposes a certain type of materiality that conditions and also makes possible any activity. From a faith perspective, the place for incarnation is the world of the poor. This does not mean an obligation—which for a university might be a practical impossibility—of physical and geographical incarnation among the poor; nor in principle is it implemented by a change of membership in the student body (although something of both could signify an adequate incarnation); nor does it imply an abandoning of specifically university methods and of the required resources. What it does mean is that the world of the poor has entered the university, that its real problems are being taken into account as something central, that social reality is being dealt with by the university and that the legitimate interests of the poor are being defended *because* they are those of the poor. How the world of the poor enters the university materially is something to be analyzed in each case; but it is important that university members be seriously interested in bringing it in, although perhaps in the form of problems, of aspirations, and of questions posed to the university. It is important that the university be also a physical space in which the poor and campesinos, grassroots persons and Amerindian leaders, can raise their voice to be heard in challenging whatever needs to be answered.

Further indicators of whether the world of the poor has entered the university are its own mode of procedure *ad extra,* its allocation of human and material resources to one or another task, more equitable distribution of financial resources among members of the university by exercising austerity and by avoiding flagrant inequalities, and a measure of austerity in the university's external undertakings.

It is unreal to think that a university must be located physically in the world of the poor, but it is imperative that it see the world from the point of view of the poor and that this world have entered the university's mind and heart. This also facilitates overcoming the temptation to worldliness by the university. Being required to use intellectual power and the necessary economic resources, being in the world together with other economic, political, and church powers that try to place it at their service, the university needs a counterweight in order to continue being relevant to the world without becoming worldly. The option for the poor is what makes possible the overcoming of that difficult danger, and without that option the balance is difficult to attain. If the university, like any other Christian institution, should be unable to fulfill the law of incarnation, it would have no viability as Christian. The option for the poor makes a Christian university possible and moreover grants it a credibility that enhances its influence in society. Because of its academic excellence, the university should have prestige; but in order to discharge adequately its social obligations, this prestige should be accompanied by a university's credibility.

The option for the poor is also useful for the exercise of the university's intellectual resources. The poor offer a light to these and specifically to theological knowledge. Although not a conclusion of natural reason, from revelation it is affirmed that in the suffering Servant of Yahweh there is light, that in Christ crucified there is wisdom. These biblical texts demand of the believer a faith reading, but they can also be read historically. The world of the poor offers a kind of light for awareness that is obtained nowhere else. Not that the world of the poor offers awareness already developed for the university, or scientific methods of research; but it does offer light. It is a light, in the first place, from the underside of history, which enables reality to be seen not only from the perspective of being and admiration, but also from that of nonbeing, from oppression and death, and from the pain and protest that these provoke; which forces knowledge to be liberative, not merely descriptive. But the world of the poor also represents a positive light, precisely for theological knowledge. The poor become a *locus theologicus,* a place of discernment of God's active presence in the world, and a place of generating a faith response to that presence — "the evangelizing potential of the poor" affirms Puebla — they become the locus of theology. From the poor, formal aspects highly important for revelation and faith are rediscovered: that the truth of revelation is good news, that God's revelation is partial, that the proclamation of the good news is carried out in an antikingdom contrary to it and against it. And from the poor, important contents of revelation are reformulated: the God of life, the good news to the poor, Christ the liberator, the church of the poor, the political dimension of love, and so forth.

It may be discussed theoretically whether the poor offer a strictly theological content matter (something discussed within the theology of liberation; see the exchange between Juan Luis Segundo and Leonardo Boff); but it is a matter beyond discussion that the poor do offer light for the reformulation of these contents and their rediscovery in the same revelation.

It is a striking fact that realities of faith today declared essential to the gospel have been ignored by theology for centuries. The Vatican instructions on liberation theology now recognize that liberation is essential to the gospel message, and nevertheless it has been absent from theology. The same might be said of the poor themselves, of the option for them, of prophetic-denunciation, of martyrdom as a Christian death, and of the effective reevaluation of central biblical passages such as Luke 4:18ff., Matthew 25, Exodus 3 and 5, the Servant of Yahweh, etc. These rediscoveries have been made by theology, but not only by doing theology. They have been made possible by a light that comes from the poor of this world. For theological knowledge—and analogously for other fields of knowledge cultivated at the university—academic excellence is an obvious necessity, which cannot be replaced by an option for the poor; but without taking account of the poor, a university can tend to degenerate into pure, sterile, and even alienating academicism; while by taking account of the poor, theology can realize its potential and become more relevant.

The option for the poor, finally, can illuminate in which sense the university should be a place of pluralism. As a social and ideological phenomenon, pluralism is a fact in the First World; as a university phenomenon, pluralism is inherent in a university, at least insofar as it consciously cultivates various fields of knowledge and, through academic freedom, takes up and even values disparity and differences. A university, as a place of pluralism, is important and beneficial. First of all because it expresses in this way that truth must be sought out and maintained, safe from dogmatism. And also because the university can offer a sign of respect and tolerance, which, above all in situations of social conflict, humanizes and permits forums for rational dialogue.

An option for the poor does not negate pluralism and its positive values, but it does place limits on pluralism. In the face of injustice, oppression and repression, there can be no institutional neutrality. The entire university should be in accord, at least morally, on a minimum standard of living for the poor. At a Christian university there may be religious, and even ideological, pluralisms; but the option for the poor should not on that account disappear. Rather it has the capacity to bring together objectively the diversity of academic fields and religious stances. The minimum that the option for the poor imposes on the university is that, in the name of pluralism, notorious aberrations not be tolerated; and the maximum is that the university as a whole, respecting legitimate pluralisms, pursue this option.

UNIVERSITY APPLICATION OF CHRISTIAN PRINCIPLES IN HISTORY

The principles explained seem to me necessary and empowering for any Christian activity and institution at all. What must be asked is whether and how a university can adopt these principles as a university. This analysis would have to be done in detail for each case; here I limit myself to enunciating the possibility as a principle.

The kingdom of God, as utopian proclamation of a new human person in a new land, can and in a Christian sense ought to constitute the horizon and finality of a university. Of its nature, a university is more akin to the kingdom's social and structural dimension, but this does not signify an abandonment in principle of the personal dimension, but takes into account that there are other places more proper to it. In fact, merely by its existence as a social force, the university already shapes society, by action and omission, along a particular line of kingdom or antikingdom.

The university is enabled to promote the kingdom actively and positively. Its scientific research can analyze rationally what constitutes, at any particular time, antikingdom, the greatest sin: what are its structural causes, what alternative models must be proposed, what steps must be taken, and the like. In addition, a method of instruction that would teach before all else the national reality (albeit with the grave difficulties mentioned above), which would orient the training of professionals to respond to the problems of national reality, would be a form of promoting the kingdom. An effective, utopian, and credible word is the basic way and method to promote the kingdom, and the same is true of the university. If on a Christian level this is the word of faith, at the university level it is the true, reasoned, and scientific word. That university word can be effective, based above all on its own rationality; it is a powerful word that can shake unjust structures when it denounces them, can offer methods and techniques for implementing the signs of the kingdom, and can influence the collective conscience in the direction of the kingdom. It is also a utopian word insofar as it proposes solutions and the best solutions, goals that are ever new and ever more fulfilling, adding to utopia the realism of means more rationally suited to its attainment.

It should also be a credible word so it can be accepted and have influence. The primary source of its credibility arises from the theoretical objectivity of its analysis, denunciations, and proposals; to which must be added what in general promotes social credibility: independence from the powers of this world, university accompaniment of the poor, the running of risks for them. This effective utopian and credible word is what can make the university reach out to society, and when this word is communicated, then the university accomplishes its function of social involvement.

The option for the poor, finally, can also be a strictly university option, although as option its roots go beyond the realm of the university. Any scientific analysis of reality certifies the immensity and cruelty of poverty; establishes its fundamentally historical nature, which is to say, based on structures created by human beings; and establishes its dialectical nature, which is to say, there are poor because there are rich, and there are rich at the expense of the poor. This latter might be a subject for discussion, although not in the Third World, and it is so recognized by the magisterium of the church.

Scientific knowledge of reality leads, therefore, at least to a serious possibility of the option for the poor, and in the Third World it leads to necessity of the option. This contains an undoubtable ethical component, but it is also a rational option guided by the same reality. Therefore the university can also make an option for the poor as a university. It can and in the Third World must be "knowledge for those who have no voice, intellectual support for those who in their reality have truth and reason, although they have been deprived of all else, but who do not have at their disposal the academic reasons to justify and legitimize their truth and their reason" (Ignacio Ellacuría). The option for the poor is not then something merely affective, although the poor may move hearts; it is not something purely ethical, although the poor may shake consciences and demand commitment; it is also something rational, and therefore can and should be an option for a university as such.

The convergence between Christian principles and the nature of the university, in the application of both in history as I have presented them from a Third World perspective, demonstrates that a Christian university is a possibility. What is Christian has no reason to do violence to a university, but can rather offer it direction and mystique, and can help it to heal the particular concupiscence and sinfulness of a university. The university has no reason to be distant from what is Christian; rather it can convert itself to being its instrument, specifically with respect to what is structural.

The historical and religious reality of Latin America demands and makes possible this type of Christian university: a university reoriented in favor of populational majorities (to use historical terms); a university reoriented in favor of the poor, of God's preferred ones (to use Christian terms). I want to add, nonetheless, although briefly, another traditional goal of the university, which in Latin America is being reevaluated too, for historical reasons. I refer to the idea that the university is a place for cultivating the spirit.

From this perspective we must recognize that in Latin America a double rediscovery has been made over recent years. On the one hand, the discovery that it is Christian to build up the kingdom, to struggle for justice, to liberate the poor majorities. This is not in discussion and is considered a most fundamental, irrevocable, and—for the foreseeable future—irreversible *conviction.* But on the other hand the need has also been felt to imbue the practice of the kingdom with spirit so that it may reach its potential and heal the inevitable negative by-products it generates. It has also been established that spirit does not arise mechanically from praxis, although the latter may promote it, but rather that spirit must be explicitly cultivated. Thus religious and social grassroots movements value more and more the cultural, the artistic, the celebrative; and the theology of liberation is developing more and more the theme of spirituality to promote a liberation with spirit.

This rediscovery, which corresponds to the nature of the human, also has significance for a Christian university as a place for cultivation of the spirit. Its decision for the kingdom from the option for the poor is already a matter of spirit and expresses the spirit of mercy, prophecy, and justice, which does not arise mechanically from purely scientific analyses. I want to refer now to other dimensions of spirit that the university can cultivate: the true and the aesthetic.

Although the university should place truth on the side of building up the kingdom, the cultivation of truth is not exhausted by it. To seek truth, to be open to it as both inspiration and critique, to let it be and to contemplate it, is something deeply humanizing and necessary. If this is done without the hubris that cripples it all, it is a way of being open to the mystery of reality and to the mystery of God, of harmonizing the activity of the search with the gratuity of the attraction. With the mystery of reality and of God, we must come into affinity and produce results, but we must also contemplate it, let it be, receive from it. The truth continues, then, to be something useful, but also more than merely useful — namely, that which humanizes human beings and prevents praxis from degenerating into pragmatism.

Cultivating the esthetic and, more generally, the sacramental and celebrative dimension of human reality is also humanizing. Through it persons express themselves, their meaning, their ideal sentiments; they find forms of communication and cohesion not achieved with merely discursive words; with it they accompany the meaning of their daily routine and the opaque moments of their history. With the esthetic and the sacramental, the mystery of reality and the mystery of God show that they are capable of evoking response, provoking action and calling persons together. The necessary rationale for praxis does not degenerate into rationalism, but becomes humanism.

The university can be, therefore, a place for cultivating the true and the beautiful, a place for contemplation and artistic expression. In this sense it can also be a place of culture, a place for cultivating and encountering cultures with their human and Christian values.

None of this, either of itself or from the point of view of the university's primary goal, is to be scorned, but rather desired. The only thing that must be added is that the contemplative, the esthetic, and the cultural are not to be understood in an elitist or classist way, and not to be used as justification for evading the university's principal goal. If the university were to act without this principal goal, the spirit would have no flesh; and if the university were to act against this goal, there would be a spirit not of life but of death. But if the university acts together with the building up of the kingdom of God, it promotes life, and life in greater abundance.

TWO MINIMUM REQUISITES FOR A CHRISTIAN UNIVERSITY

Everything expressed so far has been from the perspective of the Third World, with the hope that it may inspire a Christian university. In whatever way any of this may be possible, then what has been stated can and should be historically put into practice as something to be discerned in each case. In closing I should like to mention just two concrete points that seem important to me for any Christian university, and concern me more directly because of the theological work I am doing in a Third World country. These are some minimal requirements, but they can also be of great importance. I refer to the relationship between the university and theology, and between the university and universality.

University and Theology

A Christian university should be a place of encounter between faith and science, between faith and culture. This is necessary from the perspective of theology because the faith that underlies theology affirms that what is Christian has the capacity to inspire and bring to fullness any cultural expression and any branch of learning; and what is Christian also needs to find in these expressions ways to incarnate itself. From the perspective of culture and science, it is necessary because these offer theology demands and inquiries, but also possible purifications, — that is, contributions to the content and scientific rigor in methodology, all of which should be welcomed by theology.

But this should not mean that theology becomes disconnected from the original reality in which faith is lived, in which needs arise, as well as impulses for theology. University theology is done in the university as a physical place and as a scientific place; but it should not be done from the university as the ultimate place of inspiration. Theology should be done rather from and for the original locus of faith: the people of God. This is — as theology itself recognizes — the place where the signs of the times and the novelty of the Spirit are verified; that is, the place where the sources of theological knowledge are concretized. But it is, above all, the place of theological truth before it is the place of theology.

Theology must be turned, then, toward the people of God; it should be inserted effectively among them, draw its agenda from them and accompany them. In this sense, university theology should be a moment of theo-praxis for the whole people of God and should be considered as a theo-culture, a Christo-culture, an ecclesio-culture—that is, an instrument that cultivates and nurtures faith, hope, and love of God's people.

This does not mean, once again, that theology as a university and scientific study becomes unnecessary; on the contrary. Above all, the cultivation of theological truth and the transmitting of God's mystery continue to be important. Theologico-scientific knowledge, which illumines whence and whither the people of God is going, continues to be necessary; theologico-scientific knowledge, which relates this people's faith with the social and cultural reality in which it lives; theologico-scientific knowledge, which even overcomes the spontaneity and short-sightedness in history of this people of God. Theology, as a university discipline, can overcome certain limitations that arise from doing theology from other perspectives: clericalism, when theology is oriented unilaterally toward purely ministerial formation, and precipitous activity when there is an effort to respond only to immediate situations. University theology has, therefore, a specific function and responsibility—but within the people of God. Disconnected from them, theology's necessary responsibility before science can degenerate into sterile academics; from within and focused on the people of God, theology can help them to grow and can receive from them real impulses of faith, hope and love in order to grow itself as theology.

University and Universality

University and universality have always been interrelated. The university has considered itself a locus of the universality of learning; it has sought to be a mirror for the academic and scientific universe. Thus this universalizing perspective is natural to the university. But, to finish, I should like to propose from our deepest Christian faith another conception of the universality of the university.

Following St. Ignatius in his meditation on the incarnation, we must keep before our eyes the whole of humanity, in a variety of situations, but traveling toward perdition. Today too, real humanity finds itself on the road more to perdition than to salvation. In these days, according to United Nations' reports, the five billionth human being is to be born, and what lies ahead for this person is unemployment and malnutrition.

I would ask all universities, and specifically those of the First World, to be universal, to see the whole world and not merely their own world, to look at the world from the perspective of the Third World majorities, and not only from the exceptional islands of the First World. And I ask that, in looking at this, their hearts be moved to compassion and that they decide, as St. Ignatius says, to do salvation; that they ask themselves, as St. Ignatius did before Christ crucified: what have we done and what are we going to do for the Crucified — and for the crucified peoples?

I want to propose to you, therefore, that the universality of the university take the Third World very much into account, that the university know it, analyze it, and understand it; that the university make the Third World a fundamental perspective of its work; that it place itself at the service of the Third World; that it work, struggle, and outdo itself for the Third World's salvation, in such a way that all the subworlds may find salvation in the salvation of us all.

How the universities should do this concretely is not up to me to determine, but rather to the universities. The only thing that I should like to add is that the Third World is offering not only urgent ethical and practical demands to the universities, but that it is offering light, hope, mystique, and meaning too. To serve the Third World is to become incarnate in true humanity today; it is to recover the dignity of simply being a human person; it is to make reparation for the centuries-long sins of oppression and to experience pardon; it is to receive encouragement, hope, and grace.

To serve the Third World is to give, but it is also to receive, and to receive something of a different order from what is given and normally superior to what is given. It is to receive humanity and, for believers, to receive faith. In this giving and receiving, the university is more than addition and more than complementarity; it is mutual support and solidarity.

Every human being and every Christian — and every university too — is called to this solidarity in a world battling between life and death. If in Latin America and in Europe, in San Salvador and in Deusto, the universities listen to and gather up the sufferings and hopes of a crucified humanity, then a solidarity between the universities and through them can be established, above all a solidarity among peoples and among the human beings of this world. And then it will be a little easier for the whole of humanity to go about transforming itself into a single people with God as Father, to set out toward the kingdom of God. And when any of this occurs, it will be because the university has inspired our world, and because what is Christian has inspired the university.

— Translated by Sally Hanlon

∼ 11 ∼

Six Slain Jesuits

Joseph O'Hare, S.J.

On behalf of the Jesuits of New York Province, I welcome you to this liturgy in which through the words and signs of religious faith we celebrate our solidarity with the people of El Salvador. The occasion for our liturgy is the tragedy of last Thursday when six Jesuits and two of their household family at the Central American University in San Salvador were brutally murdered in the early morning hours. But we mourn not only for them but for all the victims of this wasteful war that for more than ten years has bled a tiny, tortured country.

We mourn for the seventy thousand persons of El Salvador who have died in this war and the hundreds of thousands who have been displaced by the fighting. We remember the martyrs who preceded last Thursday's victims, Father Rutilio Grande, a Jesuit assassinated in 1977, the same year that a rightwing paramilitary group ordered all Jesuits to leave the country or face a sentence of death. We remember Archbishop Oscar Romero, struck down by an assassin's bullet in 1980 while celebrating Mass. We remember also the four American women mission-

---

Father O'Hare is president of the Jesuit-run Fordham University in New York. His homily was delivered on November 22, 1989 at a memorial Mass at the Jesuit Church of St. Ignatius Loyola in New York. It is reprinted here from *Origins*.

aries who were kidnapped, assaulted, and murdered by military forces in December of 1980.

Our celebration today is marked by a deep sense of sorrow at the loss of human life and the cruelty of ten years of fruitless fighting. But our sorrow is based on a strong sense of solidarity with the people and the church of El Salvador. It is a solidarity based on a common faith in a God of justice, on a common mission that all Jesuits share with the Jesuits of El Salvador, and on the common identity that unites a Catholic university in El Salvador with Catholic universities throughout the world. Our sense of solidarity, however, also arises from the more troubling fact that the national policies of our two countries have been, for good or ill, inextricably linked.

And finally, our solidarity with the people of El Salvador is based on fundamental Christian hope, which declares that no matter how dark the signs of death, in the end the radiance of life will prove victorious.

Our solidarity with the people of El Salvador is based on a shared faith that this world is in the end God's world and that God is the Lord of our history. For this reason, we are committed to the cause for which the Jesuit martyrs of last Thursday died: the dignity of the human person and the kingdom of justice to which the Lord of justice calls us.

This faith in the primacy of the Lord of justice stretches beyond the divisions of race and nations to unite all of us in a common human family. It is a faith that echoes the early call of the prophet Isaiah to work to bring justice to the nations. In the words of Isaiah, the servant of the Lord "brings true justice; he will never waver, nor be crushed until true justice is established on earth. . . . I, Yahweh, have called you to serve the cause of right; I have taken you by the hand and formed you; I have appointed you as covenant of the people and light of the nations, to open the eyes of the blind, to free captives from prison, and those who live in darkness from the dungeon" (Isa 42:1).

This morning we confirm our commitment to this cause for which the Jesuits of the Central American University in El Salvador gave their lives. They were not men of violence, they were men of peace and reason. Yet they died violently. Like the servant of Yahweh, they did not cry out or shout aloud or break the crushed reed, but neither did they waver nor were they crushed. They did not leave the country in 1977 when rightwing death squads put them under a penalty of death. Nor did they leave earlier this month when government-controlled radio stations broadcast warnings against their safety. Nor will they leave now, when the attorney general of the government blames the unrest in the country on church leaders.

While these six Jesuits were struck down last Thursday, others will rise up to take their place. We pledge ourselves to the covenant with the people that cost them their lives. For us to forget them or to decide that the costs of justice are too high for us to pay would be to betray not only their memory but our faith that this is God's world and that God is the Lord of justice.

For the Jesuits assembled here this morning, our solidarity with last Thursday's martyrs has a more personal foundation as well. Many of us knew some or all of them. Several of them studied here in the United States. For my part, I remember listening to Ignacio Ellacuría during the 33rd General Congregation of the Jesuits in Rome in the fall of 1983, when he spoke with passion of the agony of his people and of the need for a response to the institutionalized violence of massive poverty and repression that crushed the vast majority of the people of El Salvador.

Father Ellacuría's words echoed the common committment of Jesuits today to serve faith and promote justice, and to see in this twofold mandate the grand intention that should inform all Jesuit works, no matter how varied. "What is it to be a companion of Jesus today? It is to engage, under the standard of the cross, in the crucial struggle of our time: the struggle for faith and that struggle for justice which it includes. . . . Thus, the way to faith and the way to justice are inseparable ways. It is on this undivided road, this steep road, that the pilgrim church must travel and toil" (*Jesuits Today,* 32nd General Congregation, 1975).

Service of faith and promotion of justice represent a contemporary expression of our Jesuit mission. The reading from St. Paul's Letter to the Corinthians that we heard this morning echoed an older statement of this mission that sums up the "sum and scope" of the Jesuit constitutions. From the very origins of the Society of Jesus nearly four hundred fifty years ago, Jesuits have declared that the character of our life (*vitae nostrae ratio*) is that Jesuits are to be "men crucified to the world and to whom the world is crucified."

How prophetic of the way these Jesuits of El Salvador lived and died are the words of St. Paul evoked in this statement of the "sum and scope" of Jesuit life: "We prove we are God's servants ... by the word of truth and by the power of God; by being armed with the weapons of righteousness in the right hand and in the left, prepared for honor or disgrace, for blame or praise; taken for imposters while we are genuine; obscure yet famous; said to be dying and here we are alive; rumored to be executed before we are sentenced; thought most miserable and yet we are always rejoicing; taken for paupers though we make others rich, for people having nothing though we have everything" (2 Cor 5:6–10).

This hymn of St. Paul to the paradoxes of the gospel has from the origins of the Society of Jesus defined our aspirations. Certainly today as we think of the Jesuit martyrs of El Salvador we can see that they were men who lived the sum and scope of our constitutions, were men crucified to the world and to whom the world was crucified, and who died promoting justice and serving faith.

For the Jesuits of the United States, most especially those working at Fordham University and at the other twenty-seven Jesuit colleges and universities in this country, there is an added sense of solidarity with the martyrs of last Thursday. This arises from the common mission we share as Jesuits working in the ministry of higher education.

In eliminating the rector and vice-rector and some of the most distinguished members of the faculty of the University of Central America, the assassins cut out the heart of one of the most respected intellectual institutions in the country. As you know from newspaper accounts, these men were not merely murdered, their brains were spilled out on the ground by their murderers, a chilling symbol of the contempt shown by men of violence for the power of truth.

There are those who have said, and who will say in the days and weeks ahead, that the Jesuits of El Salvador were not disinterested academics, that they had deliberately chosen to insert themselves into the political conflict of their nation. If they had remained within the insulated safety of the library or the class-room, their critics will charge, if they had not "meddled in pol-itics," their lives would not have been threatened.

But such a criticism misunderstands the nature of any uni-versity, and most certainly the nature of a Catholic university. No university can be insulated from the agonies of the society in which it lives. No university which identifies itself as Catholic can be indifferent to the call of the church to promote the dignity of the human person.

Pope John Paul II, himself a man from the university world, has often challenged Catholic universities to confront the crucial issues of peace and justice in our world today. On his last visit to this country in September 1987, the pope addressed a meeting of Catholic college and university presidents in New Orleans. On that occasion, he called on Catholic universities to recognize the need for the reform of attitudes and unjust structures in society. He spoke of "the whole dynamic of peace and justice in the world, as it affects East and West, North and South. . . . The parable of the rich man and the poor man is directed to the conscience of humanity, and today in particular, to the con-science of America. But that conscience often passes through the halls of academe, through nights of study and hours of prayer."

More recently, last April in his address to the Third Inter-national Congress of Catholic Universities, Pope John Paul II insisted that one of the distinguishing marks of a Catholic university must be to measure all technological discovery and all social developments in the light of the dignity of the human person.

It was this distinctive mission of a Catholic university that inspired the Jesuits of El Salvador to seek, not only through teaching and writing but also through their personal interven-tions, a resolution of the terrible conflict that has divided their land. Those of us who carry this mission of faith and justice in the relatively comfortable circumstances of North America can only be humbled by the total commitment ot the ministry of truth that stamped the lives of the Jesuit scholars and teachers of El Salvador and in the end cost them their lives.

This liturgy is not the time for political analysis or political advocacy. At the same time, we would not be faithful to the truth of this moment if we did not recognize that another more troubling source of our solidarity with the people of El Salvador is the history of the last ten years in which the government of the United States has worked closely with the government of El Salvador. Our nation's policy, in theory at least, has had respectable objectives: to control extremist forces on left and right, to encourage an environment in which the people of El Salvador can choose through democratic process the government they wish. But our government has also insisted that military assistance to the government of El Salvador is necessary to achieve these goals.

Before his assassination in 1980, Archbishop Romero had written to President Carter asking him to curtail American military aid to the government because, in Archbishop Romero's opinion, such aid only escalated the level of violence in that country and prevented the achievement of a negotiated political settlement. Now, nearly ten years later, can anyone doubt the accuracy of Archbishop Romero's warning?

At a time when our government leaders and our corporate executives hasten to socialize with the leaders of the communist giants elsewhere in the world, why must we assemble our military might to deal with the revolutionary movements in tiny Central American nations? Are our national interests really at stake? Or are we obsessed with the myth of the national security state, a myth that is discredited each day by events elsewhere in the world? After ten years of evasions and equivocations, a tissue of ambiguities, the assassinations of last Thursday pose, with brutal clarity, the question that continues to haunt the policy of the United States toward El Salvador: Can we hand weapons to butchers and remain unstained by the blood of their innocent victims?

But the final word of this liturgy cannot be one of anger or denunciation. It must be one of hope. For this too, in the end, is the final ground of our solidarity with the people of El Salvador. If Jesuits are men crucified to the world and to whom the world is crucified, it is only because we believe that out of the crucifixion of our Savior, El Salvador, came life and comes life. With the people of El Salvador we believe in the words of Jesus cited in today's gospel that "unless a wheat grain falls on the ground and dies, it remains only a single grain; but if it dies it yields a rich harvest" (John 12:24).

When Christians celebrate the eucharist they take the bread, break it and remember him who took his life, broke it and gave it that others might live. With deep hope in the resurrection of the Lord, we pray that the final word in the drama of El Salvador be one of life and hope rather than death and despair. We pray that the irony of that tiny, tortured country's name, El Salvador, the Savior, will be redeemed by the resurrection of its people.